D0923474

The Significance of Barth's Theology

The Significance of Barth's Theology

An Appraisal: With Special Reference to Election and Reconciliation

by

Fred H. Klooster

Baker Book House
Grand Rapids 6, Michigan
nineteen sixty-one

The Significance
of Barth's Theology

Library of Congress Catalog Card Number: 61-18636
Printed in the United States of America

Preface

Under the generous auspices of the Reformed Fellowship, Inc., I delivered three lectures on the theology of Karl Barth in Grand Rapids, Michigan, on September 22 and 29 and October 6, 1960. Since the lectures were scheduled shortly after my return from a sabbatical year of study at Basel, Switzerland, it was a pleasant occasion for me to present a semi-popular report of my study with the most influential theologian of our day.

I wish to record publicly my thanks to the Board of Trustees of Calvin College and Seminary for granting me sabbatical leave. To the American Association of Theological Schools I am especially grateful for a Faculty Fellowship which enabled me to carry out a project of study and research at Basel, Switzerland. The University of Basel graciously offered me full use of its rich facilities, and it was a privilege to be present during the celebrations of this venerable institution's five hundredth anniversary. Professor Karl Barth was very kind in allowing me to participate in all of his academic activities, an average of eight hours per week, for two semesters. And he freely offered himself for personal contact when desired. I have attempted to be objective in my presentation of his thought. Although I have found myself in basic disagreement with his theology, this disagreement results from an attempt to evaluate Barth's thought by the sole criterion by which he acknowledges that he wishes to be judged, namely, the Holy Scriptures.

I wish to thank the Reformed Fellowship, Inc. for the invitation to deliver these lectures as well as for undertaking to publish them now in book form.

Grand Rapids, Michigan

Fred H. Klooster

Foreword

The three chapters of this book deal with important aspects of the theology of Karl Barth. They have their origin in a series of lectures on that subject by the author, Dr. Fred H. Klooster, professor of Systematic Theology at Calvin Seminary, and were delivered at Calvin College Chapel on three successive Thursday evenings in the early Fall of 1960. They were given soon after Dr. Klooster had returned from a full year's stay in Basel, Switzerland, where he was in almost daily contact with Dr. Barth, attending lectures, seminars, and colloquia. This, as well as the keen interest which Barth's views have awakened and the profound influence which they have exerted in theological circles, accounted for the eagerness with which many looked forward to these lectures. Notwithstanding the complex and abstruse nature of Barth's system of thought, Dr. Klooster has succeeded admirably in giving a lucid presentation of that theology, particularly its construction of the doctrines of divine election and reconciliation, and of his own evaluation of Barth's views.

The lectures which this book presents were carefully revised by the author. They were delivered and are now published under the auspices of Reformed Fellowship, Inc., publishers of the magazine *Torch and Trumpet.*

REFORMED FELLOWSHIP, INC.
Grand Rapids, Michigan

Contents

Chapter I

The Significance of Karl Barth's Theology

Chapter I

The Significance of Karl Barth's Theology

Why is Karl Barth's theology significant today? Among the various reasons that could be adduced, the following certainly deserve consideration. Karl Barth has 1) influenced the entire theological situation of our generation, 2) led the theological revolt against liberalism, 3) awakened a new interest in Scripture, 4) inspired a new interest in the Reformers, especially Calvin, and 5) developed a new theology, the comprehensive system of thought set forth in his monumental *Die kirchliche Dogmatik.* In this chapter an attempt will be made to sketch these reasons for Barth's importance, and then to present a brief evaluation of Barth's theology.

A. Reasons for the Significance of Barth's Theology.

1. *The Most Influential Theologian of This Generation.*

No matter how one may finally evaluate the theology of Karl Barth, the influence which his thought has had during the past forty years is astounding. It is itself a unique achievement for a theologian to determine the theological climate and to be at the center of theological debate during four decades of his own lifetime. Such considerations have led T. F. Torrance of Edinburgh to declare that "Karl Barth is incontestably the greatest figure in modern theology since Schleiermacher, occupying an honored position among the great elite of the church – Augustine, Anselm, Aquinas, Luther and Calvin."[1] Although this judgment reveals Torrance's strong attachment to Barth's theology, and although one may

[1]"Karl Barth" in *Ten Makers of Modern Protestant Thought,* ed. by George L. Hunt (New York: Association Press, 1958), p. 58.

legitimately question whether Barth should be classed with Augustine, Luther and Calvin, there can be no doubt that Barth has dominated the twentieth century as Schleiermacher dominated the nineteenth.

Recognition of the influence of Barth's thought has come from opponents as well as admirers in various communions. G. Gloege, a Lutheran opponent, regards Barth's dogmatics as the most important systematic theology of this century.[2] With greater sympathy for Barth's theology, W. Matthias views the publication of Barth's *Church Dogmatics* as the beginning of a new epoch in evangelical theology.[3] And even Roman Catholics have not escaped Barth's influence. A French Catholic theologian, H. Boulliard, speaks of Barth's work as a Copernican revolution in Protestant theology which put an end to the dominance of liberal thought. Boulliard also adds that Roman Catholics should rejoice because Barth has again restored to Protestant theology an emphasis upon the sovereignty of God's Word and the primacy of Jesus Christ as the Son of God.[4]

Although this first point, on the significant influence of Barth's theology, is primarily a formal consideration, it is interesting to illustrate it more fully. The past tension-full decades have seen many theologians change their positions. The famous liberal magazine, *The Christian Century*, has documented these changes each decade in an interesting series entitled, "How My Mind Has Changed." The reader will immediately recognize Barth's influence as he sees these religious and theological leaders repeatedly refer to Karl Barth to describe their own individual pilgrimages. In the current series John C. Bennett and Reinhold and H. Richard Niebuhr amply illustrate the point.

John C. Bennett, Dean of Union Theological Seminary

---

[2]*Religion in Geschichte und Gegenwart,* Dritte Auflage, Bd. I (Tübingen: J.C.B. Mohr, 1957), col. 895.

[3]*Evangelisches Kirchenlexicon,* Bd. I (Göttingen: Vandenhoeck & Ruprecht, 1956), col. 323.

[4]*Lexikon für Theologie und Kirche,* Zweiter Auflage, Bd. II (Freiburg: Herder, 1958) col. 7.

and a close associate of Reinhold Niebuhr, states that while he has "always been a critic of Karl Barth," he is surprised to find himself learning so much from Barth in recent years.[5] Bennett voices his appreciation of Barth's "form of Christian humanism" which means that the "fall" of Adam "is already neutralized, indeed overcome, by Christ, and that man, even as we know him, is to be understood in the light of Christ rather than in the light of fallen Adam."[6] Due to Barth's "massive reiteration" Bennett has grasped "the revolutionary nature of the revelation of God in Christ," i.e. "the way in which all of our understanding of God's ultimate attributes must be understood in the light of his coming into this sinful and finite human world in Christ."[7] Thus Bennett finds himself learning much from Barth, although he warns that followers of Barth must be careful lest they neglect the other disciplines of study and culture and fall into some form of obscurantism.

The Niebuhr brothers also acknowledge the influence of Barth's theology as they indicate their changes in thought during the past decade. H. Richard Niebuhr of Yale Divinity School admits that he had followed Barth in the reaction to liberal theology and has also heard himself labelled a Barthian. However, H. Richard Niebuhr now wishes to dissociate himself from Barth's theology and acknowledges a growing interest in the "empirical and ethical strain in theology" which is basic to the intentions of Rudolf Bultmann.[8] He finds himself moving away from "Barth and the dogmatic biblical theology current today in wide circles," and claims to have discovered more "kinship with all theologians of Christian experience than with the theologians of Christian doctrine."[9] H. Richard Niebuhr sums up his general evaluation of Barth's influence today in these words: "I believe

---

[5]*The Christian Century*, LXXVI, 51 (Dec. 23, 1959), p. 1500.

[6]*Ibid.*, p. 1501.

[7]*Ibid.*

[8]"Reformation: Continuing Imperative," *The Christian Century*, LXXVII, 9 (March 2, 1960), pp. 248, 250.

[9]*Ibid.*, p. 250.

that the Barthian correction of the line of march begun ir Schleiermacher's day was absolutely essential, but that it ha become an overcorrection and that Protestant theology car minister to the church's life more effectively if it resumes th general line of march represented by the evangelical, empirica and critical movement."[10]

And even Reinhold Niebuhr, who recently retired as Vic President of Union Theological Seminary in New York acknowledges Barth's major influence in contemporary theol ogy, although he declares that Barth has now become ir relevant to responsible Christians in the West and has ceasec to have any effect on his own thought. Reinhold Niebuh does admit that Barth is "something of a genius" who possesse "more imagination than any other living theologian."[11] Bu Niebuhr, whose major interest has centered in questions o social ethics, rather than in those of dogmatic theology, now writes off Barth completely—although he thereby indicate that he cannot simply ignore Barth. He states: "What began then, as a creative religious movement restoring the evangelica and prophetic power to the church and enabling it to speak a word of judgment to the pretensions of nations, culture and civilizations—ended as a complicated eschatological sys tem offering a stance from which one could hurl anathema against both the communists and Western democracies. Thus Barth could accuse both America and West Germany of re sembling the 'fleshpots of Egypt' and fellow Christians, who tried to preserve a responsible attitude toward the treasure of Western civilization and the perils of nuclear catastrophe, of being Western 'politicians' in disguise."[12] Then Reinhold Niebuhr goes on to make this devastating evaluation of Barth's position:

> Barth's assumption that the price of religious and propheti detachment from the illusions of our culture must be the accept ance of his whole eschatological system may be regarded a

---

[10]*Ibid.*

[11]"The Quality of Our Lives," *The Christian Century,* **LXXVII, 1** (May 11, 1960), p. 570.

[12]*Ibid.,* p. 571.

> either the inevitable egotism of a very great man or as the consequence of the degeneration to a system of a religiously creative attitude. What 17th-century Lutheran orthodoxy did to Luther in a century, Barth managed to do to his own thought in a few decades. What was left unfinished was supplied by the epigoni who have developed a new Scholasticism on Barth's foundations. I record these developments without too much animus because Barth has long since ceased to have any effect on my thought; indeed he has become irrelevant to all Christians in the Western world who believe in accepting the common and collective responsibilities without illusion and without despair. We cannot protect the truth of the gospel by separating it from all the disciplines of culture and all the common experiences of our ethical life.[13]

The quotations from Bennett and the two Niebuhrs indicate the importance Barth's theology has had upon contemporary theology, even though there are significant indications of a movement on the part of some from Barth to Bultmann.

Sufficient evidence has been presented to illustrate the significance of Barth's theology today. L. Harold De Wolf sums it up well:

> There is no doubt that Karl Barth has made a stronger impact upon Protestant theology than any other man of the twentieth century, thus far. So varied and far-reaching is his influence that whether one welcomes his ideas or opposes them one cannot ignore them and still gain even an elementary understanding of the present situation in theology.[14]

If the seminary student, the minister, the intelligent church member is to be alert to the religious thinking of our day, he cannot ignore the theology of Karl Barth. Barth has placed his stamp upon our age, and, like it or not, we are compelled to come to grips with his thought.

2. *The Theological Revolt against Liberalism.*

The so-called neo-orthodox reaction to Liberalism was spearheaded by Karl Barth. The strangle-hold of the liberal theology of Schleiermacher and Ritschl has been broken, at least

---

[13] *Ibid.*

[14] *Present Trends in Christian Thought* (New York: Association Press, 1960), p. 78 f.

in part, by Barth's leadership. From its inception, Barth's theology has been a theology of reaction, and the precise nature of the reaction has been determined by the opponent of the moment. This is not only a reason for Barth's theological importance, but it also adds a complicating factor to an understanding of his theology.

Karl Barth's personal history is, in this respect, largely the theological history of an entire generation. The theology of Schleiermacher controlled the nineteenth century. Adapted by Albrecht Ritschl, this liberal theology entered the twentieth century in the form of the history, psychology, and philosophy of religion. Its chief proponents were Adolf von Harnack, Wilhelm Herrmann, and Ernst Troeltsch. Liberal theology in this form was really a cultural anthropology, for it replaced God and his revelation with man and his religious experiences. In place of the gospel of redemption for lost sinners, it stressed a social gospel for men innately good.

Barth came to know this theology first hand from its chief representatives and adopted it as his own. Not only was he an avid reader and admirer of Schleiermacher, but he also studied with Harnack at Berlin and Herrmann at Marburg. At Marburg Barth also became acquainted with the Neo-Kantian philosophers H. Cohen and P. Natorp. Barth was eager to make a good impression upon Harnack during his seminar in Berlin, but it was especially Harnack who later was driven to anger by the theology of the *Römerbrief*.

After his theological study was completed, Barth began his ministry as the assistant pastor of the German Reformed congregation in historic Geneva. Here he made further study of the life and thought of the great Reformer of Geneva, John Calvin. But the real break with liberalism was not to come until Barth moved to the obscure village of Safenwil in the Canton Aargau. Here he remained for ten years (1911-1921) and passed through the turbulent period of the First World War. Each Sunday he faced his congregation in a little white church perched on the side of a hill overlooking the sleepy industrial village less than fifty miles from Basel and Zürich, and about forty miles south of the German frontier. Gradually

Barth's reaction to liberalism came to expression. He began o realize that liberalism had followed a blind alley, and that his own liberal message did not meet the needs of the congregation during a time of war. It came as a shock to him o learn that some of his esteemed teachers should endorse he German war aims, and he came to realize that a defective ethics must stem from an inadequate theology. Such experiences led Barth and his neighboring pastor, Eduard Thurneysen, to reread the Scriptures and to study the writngs of the Reformers. Out of this context in 1919 came Barth's *Römerbrief,* a commentary on Paul's Epistle to the Romans. The second edition appeared in 1921 and this horoughly reworked edition catapulted Barth into internaional prominence. Since then Barth has been at the center of the theological debates. Therefore the year 1919 or 1921 s generally regarded as the beginning of this new era in Protestant theology, and the *Römerbrief* was its original manifesto.

For us it is especially interesting to recall that this was not he first reaction to liberalism that was voiced in Europe. n another small country the reaction had been expressed much earlier and more positively. In the Netherlands the great Reformatory movement had begun many years before hrough the *Afscheiding* of 1834 and the *Doleantie* of 1890. By the time Barth's second *Römerbrief* appeared (1921), the earthly labors of both Abraham Kuyper and Herman Bavinck were finished. Their influence, unfortunately, was largely confined to Holland and to a language to which the rest of he world had little access. But the reaction to liberalism made rom the land of the Alps was heard round the world. How trange the providence of God! How much we would have preferred the echoes from Amsterdam and Kampen to have esounded to the four corners of the world. What a different cene we might now be facing if that movement had set the one for the theological discussions of our day. We shall have to reckon with the fact, however, that it was not the eformatory voice from the Low Countries, but the voice of eaction from the Jura and the Alps that was to receive a hearing in this era, and to complicate it too.

The power of Barth's reaction to liberalism came in part from the fact that it arose from within the very bosom of liberalism itself. Furthermore, the time for it was ripe. It was not simply the nature of Barth's reaction that gave it wide hearing. The fact that Barth's experiences were also those of many other pastors and theologians provided immediate interest in what he said and wrote. The liberal message of progress through human effort was simply no message for a world at war. The subjectivism of Liberalism had put man in the place of God. And so Barth challenged his contemporaries with the theme: let God be God, and let man learn again how to be man, instead of trying to be as God. Barth declared that the supreme sin was the attempt of religious man, man in his religion, to twist the truth to suit his own selfish ends. True, this challenging reaction did lead some liberals, as Harnack, to anger and violent resistance. But in general it was a reaction that struck a responsive chord in many religious leaders whose unhappy experiences with liberalism were similar to those of Barth.

Barth's theological significance began, then, with his revolt against regnant liberal theology of his day. But this reactionary note has remained a dominant characteristic of Barth's theology. The reader can best understand the particular emphasis of Barth's thought if he is aware of the particular opponent Barth has in mind at that moment. Even Barth's major work, the *Church Dogmatics,* is not systematic in the same sense as the systematic theologies of the classic Reformed theologians. Later I will seek to show that Barth's theology does actually involve a "system" of thought, in another sense. It is important, however, to recognize that there is always something of an *occasional* character to Barth's writing. At first he claimed to be writing only a "marginal note" to theology, or simply to be supplying the salt or seasoning. Even today he insists that every dogmatics is immediately in need of rewriting since the situation always changes.

The occasional and reactionary character of Barth's writing must always be recognized. He seeks constantly to overthrow the positions of his two great enemies, liberalism on the left and orthodoxy on the right. His later writings also show the reaction to those who separated from the original movement, such as Brunner, Gogarten, and Bultmann. The whole of volume four, for example, involves the theme of reconciliation in which Barth admits that he is engaged in an intensive debate with Rudolf Bultmann, even though the latter's name rarely appears. Then again a section of the *Church Dogmatics* may be determined by his opposition to the Roman Catholic position or the Lutheran–Calvinistic differences. Time and time again during my study in Basel, pages of Barth's *Church Dogmatics* became more intelligible when it became clear whose position was before the author's mind at the time of writing. In that light one could sometimes understand why certain elements which one would normally expect to find there were absent, though not necessarily denied by Barth. The occasion of the moment dictated what was to be included then. And a later occasion might call for emphasizing precisely the element formerly in the background. At one time Barth may find it necessary to stress "grace *in the judgment*" while at a later time it is the "*grace* in the judgment" which demands emphasis.[15] Again, at one time it is the *deity* of God that requires attention, and later it may be the *humanity* of God that calls for clarification.[16] In general it may be said that earlier Barth was more interested in polemic and negation, while he now wishes to place greater emphasis upon the positive. This reactionary note, however, still runs through all of Barth's writings. He does not desire to set forth the biblical teaching in a comprehensive or systematic way. He emphatically denies the possibility of a system of theology in the sense of the great Reformed writers. Of course, I do not mean to imply that Reformed theology should not engage in polemics, that is, in the refutation of errors of all kinds and of one-sided emphases as well. It is important and necessary that Reformed dogmatics continually

---

[15]G. C. Berkouwer, *The Triumph of Grace in the Theology of Karl Barth.* (Grand Rapids: Eerdmans, 1956), p. 49.

[16]Karl Barth, *The Humanity of God* (Richmond: John Knox Press, 1960), p. 37.

indicate its distinctiveness and refute the many erroneous positions that claim men's attention. Important and necessary as this function may be, however, it should not dictate the form of one's dogmatics.

In view of what I have called the reactionary note in Barth's theology, i.e. the particular occasion determining the emphasis of the moment, it may be well to caution against the all too common idea in this country that Barth is forever changing his mind. There has certainly been an unusual amount of change on Barth's part—far more than is common in influential theologians. What a contrast, for example, between Calvin and Barth on this score! Barth has, without doubt, undergone some basic changes. The most important of these was the change from the liberal position in which he had been trained to the reaction of the *Römerbrief*. The change from 1919 to 1921 demanded the complete rewriting of the *Römerbrief*. Then came the single volume of *Die christliche Dogmatik* in 1927 which had to undergo a complete revision in content as well as in title. But since the appearance of the first volume of *Die kirchliche Dogmatik* in 1932 there has been a line of continuity to the present. This continuity, it is true, is not one of complete identity. However, Barth contends with a good deal of justification that after his break with liberalism as signalized in the revised *Römerbrief*, there has been the simple attempt to express more accurately what he really meant in the first place. While today he stresses the positive aspect more, this is simply the corollary of the original negative. While today he stresses grace rather than judgment, or the humanity rather than the deity of God, this is simply to emphasize the correlative aspect of what was maintained earlier but did not need emphasis then.

The much discussed lecture on the *Humanity of God* is a good illustration of the point.[17] This lecture has been widely hailed as a major turn in the direction of Barth's thought, a new change of mind. Barth admits that in speaking on this theme he is suggesting *a change of direction*.[18] It is important

[17] *Ibid.*
[18] *Ibid.*, p. 37.

to note, however, that he uses the mild term *Wendung* rather than *Umkehr*. The change in 1919 involved what Barth would call an *Umkehr,* a 180 degree turn of the rudder. But the change of direction involved in speaking of "the humanity of God" means a change which is not in opposition to, but only distinguished from, an earlier change.[19] Note how Barth explains the matter:

> Unmistakably for us the *humanity* of God at that time moved from the center to the periphery, from the emphasized principal clause to the less emphasized subordinate clause. I should indeed have been somewhat embarrassed if one had invited me to speak on the humanity of God—say in the year 1920, the year in which I stood up in this hall against my great teacher, Adolf von Harnack. We should have suspected evil implications in this topic. In any case we were not occupied with it. That is our subject for today and that I could not refuse to say something on it is a symptom of the fact that that earlier change of direction was not the last word. It could not be. Similarly, the change in which we are now engaged cannot be the last word. That however, may become the concern of another generation.[20]

As Barth views these changes he could still write as he did in 1939 that "the thing that changed was not I, but the situation."[21] Thus he asserts that he is conscious only of "having walked further on the way which I had begun."[22] Or to put it in the more humorous expression of a later writing, he can say:

> See the moon in yonder sky?
> 'Tis only half that meets the eye.[23]

In order to understand the significance of Karl Barth's theology, it is important, then, to remember that it is characterized throughout by the reactionary note. The first and major reaction was the revolt against liberalism. But this reactionary feature continues to put its stamp upon all of Barth's work, and is prominent even in his most systematic work, the *Church Dogmatics*.

---

[19] *Ibid.*

[20] *Ibid.*, p. 38.

[21] *The Christian Century*, LVI, 38 (Sept. 20, 1939), p. 1133.

[22] *Ibid.*, LVI, 37 (Sept. 13, 1939), p. 1098.

[23] *The Humanity of God*, p. 42.

3. *The New Interest in the Bible.*

Barth's theology has a unique appeal to orthodox Christians because it claims to be a theology of the Word of God. Over against the older liberalism, Barth stressed man's need of revelation, and he appealed to Scripture as a witness to revelation. Largely through the influence of Barth, a group of theologians have come to call themselves "biblical theologians." Although his thought has been described as dialectical theology, theology of crisis, Barthianism, new modernism, neo-orthodoxy, theology of the triumph of grace, Barth rejects all of these terms. He prefers but one name, Theology of the Word of God. And he asserts that he wishes to be judged by just one standard or criterion—namely, Scripture.

The fact that Barth and Thurneysen discovered what they called a "strange new world"[24] in the Bible, proves how alien the message of the Scripture had become to this generation of liberals. It is a fact that Barth has given a great deal of attention to Scripture. His commentaries on Romans, Corinthians and Philippians indicate this as well as the long exegetical sections in the various volumes of the *Church Dogmatics.* Through the influence of Barth an amazing amount of study has been devoted to the Bible, and this has produced new lexicons, commentaries, Bible dictionaries and biblical theologies. Even for the orthodox scholar, many side benefits have resulted from these labors. However, the real nature of these biblical studies leaves much to be desired, a point to which I shall return in my evaluation of Barth's theology.

One feature of this new interest in the Bible demands our attention here. Along with the new emphasis upon so-called biblical theology, there has gone a disparagement of systematic theology. That is not to deny that increased effort has been put forth to produce works in dogmatics. Contemporary theologians have been producing many theological works of the type which the liberal scholars regarded as useless labor.

---

[24]Cf. "The Strange New World Within the Bible," *The Word of God and the Word of Man,* trans. by Douglas Horton (New York: Harper Torchbook, 1957), pp. 28-50.

In fact Barth's *Church Dogmatics,* of which twelve massive volumes have already appeared, is no doubt the most extensive dogmatics of all time. But Barth and those influenced by him have challenged the legitimacy of systematic theology in the sense of Kuyper, Bavinck or C. Hodge. Otto Weber has put the matter clearly when he says, "there can be no system, since God's truth is not given to us as a principle but as a Person. . . . A system is possible only under the tacit assumption of the real possession of grace. . . . Theology of the Word must constantly remain open."[25] Underlying this new interest in Scripture is actually a *new view* of Scripture, which seeks something of a synthesis between the orthodox and the liberal view of Scripture. While there is a concern to use the Scriptures, the position of higher criticism is held to be valid. And it is this approach to the Scripture which actually vitiates the basic gains that one might expect from the renewed interest in the Bible.

It is imperative that we recognize that the study of Scripture and the pursuit of exegesis is not itself a guarantee that the Biblical message is really heard. Exegesis, no less than dogmatics, involves human work, and the work of man is always sinful and subject to error. The presuppositions of the exegete as well as the presuppositions of the dogmatician are all-important. And false presuppositions with respect to the nature and unity of the Scripture may preclude a genuine hearing of the biblical message. We all know this to be true of the Roman Catholic, Arminian and Liberal theologians. But we must not fail to realize that it is true also of neo-orthodox theologians today. The choice between a biblical theology and a systematic theology, as that choice is frequently put today, rests upon a false dilemma. Genuinely Reformed systematic theology is truly biblical. And much of the self-designated "biblical theology" of neo-orthodox theologians is not genuinely biblical. Much of the contemporary form of biblical theology involves exegetical and lexical studies based upon the theological positions of Barth or Bultmann.

---

[25]*Grundlagen der Dogmatik,* Bd. I (Neukirchen, Moers: Verlag der Buchhandlung des Erziehungsverein, 1955), p. 77.

Most of the benefits that we shall reap from the current studies will be in small details rather than in the main lines of thought. And these benefits can be garnered, moreover only if we properly discriminate and discern.

There is much more that ought to be said on this point for it is an important one. But perhaps enough has been indicated to demonstrate that another reason for the significance of Barth's theology consists in the fact that he has awakened a new interest in Scripture.

4. *The New Interest in Calvin.*

Another appealing reason for the significance of Barth's theology arises from the fact that he has awakened a new interest in the Reformers and especially in Calvin. Barth has not been the only theologian responsible for the renascence of Reformation studies, but he has probably done more than any other for the particular interest in the writings of Calvin.

When Barth as a young liberal minister began searching for a more solid basis for preaching, he turned to the Scriptures and also to the writings of the Reformers. Already during his stay in Geneva, but especially during his ministry at Safenwil, he became aware of the relevance of Calvin's theology. Since then the interest in the Reformers has continued unabated.

Barth is frank to admit that he does not find Calvin's thought congenial at every point. He openly rejects Calvin's doctrine of election and substitutes a radically new doctrine, as I hope to indicate in the second chapter. On the other hand, it can not be said that Barth really accepts the basic views of Calvin while differing only at certain points. Barth's understanding of Calvin is radically different from the way Calvin has been understood by Reformed teachers and authors. Barth's use of Calvin is often one that appeals to Calvin's words, but actually involves a reinterpretation of Calvin's doctrine. His appeal to Calvin in support of his view of Scripture is an outstanding instance of such reinterpretation.

Nevertheless, Barth has been instrumental in rekindling a widespread interest in Calvin. This new interest has already led to the republication and retranslation of Calvin's writings. New studies on various phases of Calvin's thought have been published. New translations of the *Institutes* have appeared in French, German, Dutch and just recently in English. The commentaries and tracts of Calvin are being issued in new, up-to-date translations. In Japan a Calvin Translation Society is at work translating the writings both of Calvin and of Barth. And, no doubt, this reawakened interest in Calvin is only beginning to show its results.

What must we think of all this? It strikes me, first of all, as an indictment of ourselves. We who pride ourselves on our Calvinistic heritage have made almost no contribution to this Calvin renascence. Not only did we fail to contribute to the reawakened interest in Calvin, but now that it has taken place, we have failed to make any major contribution to it.

In spite of this failure on our part, I am convinced that we now face a challenge which we may not ignore. The liberal theology produced a climate which was not at all congenial to Calvin's world-and-life view. It was, indeed, openly hostile to it. Perhaps it was that liberal atmosphere which partially stifled our own interest and publication. But no such excuse exists today. Although Calvin's thought is not really congenial to our age, there is an amazing interest in it. Everyone of us should face that challenge by seeking for a deeper and more alert awareness of Calvin's writings. We can not expect to make an impact on the present scene unless we know Calvin thoroughly from his own sources. More than that, we need to learn anew to appreciate Calvin and the significance of his work. For Calvin produced a biblical theology in the true sense of the word. It is biblical thought which is warmly organized and systematized in his classic *Institutes,* a work which Calvin wished to be used alongside of his many commentaries.

It is also incumbent upon us to become better acquainted with the many works about Calvin now appearing on the market. We must be alert to their frequently neo-orthodox background and presuppositions. The future of orthodox

Calvinism is itself at stake. What is sorely needed is solid work in our own circles—work which, when published, will certainly gain a hearing today. There is a great need, and a challenge second to none, to contribute sound interpretations of Calvin to the interested public of today. This challenging situation which we now face is in large measure due to Karl Barth who has awakened a new interest in Calvin's theology.

5. *The New Theology of Karl Barth.*

Thus far I have sketched the significance of Barth in a rather formal way. I have pointed to his significance as the most influential theologian of our day, as the leader of the revolt against liberalism, as one concerned for a theology of the Word of God, and as one who has inspired a new interest in Calvin. These formal factors are important in themselves, but we have yet to indicate the real nature of the significance of Barth. That which underlies these points of interest and actually binds them together is the new theology which Barth has developed.

Barth's *Church Dogmatics* presents a new, unique, and complex theological system of thought. The term "system of theology" has become the target of widespread criticism today, as noted above. Barth has himself been one of the most vigorous critics of systems of theology. All along he has claimed to produce only a marginal note or a corrective for theology, but not a system. He has repeatedly asserted that a system of theology is neither possible nor legitimate. Now, it must be admitted that genuine Reformed theology never did attempt to develop a *closed* system of thought. Its purpose was simply to set forth in an integral unity the system of thought presented in the Scripture. It is true that a certain scholasticism has invaded also Reformed theology, especially in the 17th century. However, this was itself a partial deformation of the true Reformed theology of Calvin. And even Calvin was not without fault in this respect. Nor were Kuyper and Bavinck, in spite of their tremendous contributions, entirely free from criticism on this score. But systematic theology in the sense in which it was pursued by

Calvin, Kuyper, and Bavinck is not only possible but necessary and mandatory. Their systematic theologies did not aim at a *closed* system. Nor did they seek to produce a system of theology by means of logical deduction from a few given principles. Rather, they sought believingly to reproduce and systematize the revelation of God as this is given to us by the Scriptures. The basic opposition to systematic theology in this sense stems today from a view of Scripture which is radically different from that of Calvin, Kuyper, and Bavinck. As one grasps the roots of that difference, he will better understand the fundamental attacks that are being made upon systematic theology.

Now, it is interesting to note that although Barth, and contemporary thought in general, is opposed to a system of theology, Barth has himself devised the most original and imposing system of theology of our day. *Die kirchliche Dogmatik* sets forth this massive, interrelated system of thought. In the third chapter I will try to describe one significant part of that system as it shows itself in the doctrine of reconciliation. Here it is possible to indicate only the main features of it. At the center of this system is Barth's concept of Jesus Christ. The single source and norm of all Barth's thought is his view of Jesus Christ, and from this source he draws all sorts of deductions for the whole of his system. The Scripture is simply the witness to that revelation, but the revelation itself is said to be Jesus Christ.

In the light of that principle of Jesus Christ, Barth attempts to rethink the past history of dogmatics and rework it himself. His thought does have significant connections with the past, and his vast knowledge of the Reformers and the 17th century theologians probably contributes to at least the formal similarity of his treatment of basic themes. The actual result, however, is significantly different, and that according to his own assertion. But Barth's theology involves a system, one that is not genuinely rooted in the Scripture but read into the Scripture in terms of the basic principles of his Christology.

One of the most famous German existentialist philosophers, Karl Jaspers, also teaches at the University of Basel. Near the conclusion of his recent course on "Philosophic Faith in Relation to Christian Revelation," Jaspers paid a remarkable tribute to Karl Barth. Jaspers indicated that while he and many of his associates are making only scattered contributions to scientific thought, the really great significance of Karl Barth lies in the fact that he has thought through the whole field of theology and reworked it for himself. This I understood to be a tacit acknowledgment that Barth was really producing something of a system of thought.

It is here that we come to the major significance of Karl Barth—the new theological position which he has set forth. It is a theology which was formed in the context of a revolt against liberalism while it makes its appeal to Scripture and to the Reformers. We must now attempt a brief evaluation of the main lines of this new theology which has made Barth so significant in our day.

B. Evaluation.

The significance of Barth's theology can hardly be exaggerated. But what are we to think of the theology of this influential Swiss theologian? How shall we evaluate his significance in the light of the Scriptures as the inspired and infallible Word of God? Is the appearance of Barth's theology an unmixed blessing? Or does it harbor perilous dangers for the Church of Jesus Christ? Does it set forth the Biblical message which really meets man's tragic need?

In considering this question I am reminded of Professor A. D. R. Polman's sketch of the significance of Abraham Kuyper's theology.[26] Polman indicates three basic convictions which characterized all of Kuyper's theological activity. First and foremost, there was the deep conviction that Holy Scripture as the Word of God has absolute authority and is therefore the only source and norm of all theology. Secondly, Kuyper had no desire to form a new school of thought or to push his own personality into the foreground, but wished simply to build upon the Confessional basis of the fathers.

---

[26]*Christelijke Encyclopedie,* Tweede Druk, Bd. IV (Kampen: J. H. Kok, 1959), pp. 350-351.

However, such building upon the Reformed Confessions could not be a mere revival of the old or an unconditional submission to the authority of ancient men. Rather, the Confession for which the fathers had given their life-blood had to become the confession of their children by way of personal conviction. Therefore Kuyper sought to restate Reformed theology in the language of his day, to explain it more fully, to set it forth in a more satisfactory context, and to safeguard it against the current heresies. Thirdly, Kuyper wished theology to be of service to the Church of Jesus Christ. The fruits of theology should be made available in an understandable form to the entire church. Although these characteristics are used by Polman to describe Kuyper's theological activity, they are also applicable to Herman Bavinck and other great Reformed theologians. I should like to evaluate Karl Barth's theology with respect to these three features.

At numerous points Barth's theology resembles traditional Reformed thought. In fact, Barth's theology might be characterized by these same three characteristics which Polman used to describe the theological activity of Abraham Kuyper.[27] This would, however, be primarily a surface similarity. Let us evaluate the theology of Barth in the light of these three characteristics.

1. The recognition of the absolute authority of Scripture is fundamental to Reformed theology. Although the precise nature of the authority of Scripture in Barth's theology is problematic, and the ground for Scripture's authority according to Barth's theology is not its inspiration, it must be admitted that Barth has given Scripture an important place in his thought. No one can deny that many people have begun to read the Scriptures again as a result of Barth's influence upon them. It is possible that some people have returned to a genuinely biblical faith as a result of this renewed interest in the Scriptures. This may have happened to some who were previously liberals as well as to some members of Reformed churches which had unfortunately fallen into the stupor of dead orthodoxy. These possibilities should not close

---

[27]Cf. T. F. Torrance, *op. cit.*, pp. 63-65.

our eyes, however, to the fact that Barth's view of Scripture is not genuinely Reformed.

Barth's theology accepts the higher critical view of Scripture. The so-called scientific findings of liberalism are regarded as valid. The inspiration of Scripture is rejected, and hence the genuine basis for its authority is likewise rejected by Barth. He does not accept the self-attestation of Scripture, and when one does not accept Scripture's testimony to itself, the authority of Scripture is not fully acknowledged. There can be no doubt or misunderstanding on this score. Barth explicitly denies that Scripture is the *inspired* Word of God.[28] According to Barth, inspiration pertains to the reader of Scripture, not the writer or the writing. There is no small difference here between Barth and orthodoxy. There is an unbridgeable gulf. Barth denies that the Scriptures are the very Word of God. He denies the infallibility of Scripture. In fact, he asserts that the entire Bible is a human fallible document and to seek for infallible parts in Scripture is "mere self-will and disobedience."[29] There should be no confusion on this crucial matter. Barth has never changed his position on this subject.

In spite of the formal similarity between Barth and Kuyper, Bavinck, or Calvin in the appeal to Scripture, there is a world of difference. There can be no genuinely Reformed theology when the true authority of the inspired Scripture is not confessed. It may be added, of course, that a firm acknowledgment of the authority of Scripture does not itself guarantee a genuinely Reformed theology. Every Reformed theologian as well as every Reformed believer must always be alert to the tremendous responsibility of listening to the Word of God. It is not an easy task to bring every thought into captivity unto Jesus Christ. Part of such obedience, however, is involved in the acceptance of Scripture's own witness to its inspiration. This was acknowledged in the theology of Kuyper, but it is denied in the theology of Barth.

2. A second point of comparison and evaluation concerns

---

[28]*Church Dogmatics,* I/2 (New York: Scribner, 1956), pp. 457 ff.
[29]*Ibid.,* p. 531.

the question of a genuine return to the historical roots of the Reformation and the Reformed Confessions. When men like Kuyper and Bavinck appealed to the theology of the Reformers and to the Reformed Confessions, they did more than simply return to the past. Linking themselves to the important line of history, they also made significant advance in Reformed theology. Their work was also reformatory in character; they were prophetic theologians.

We have noted earlier that Karl Barth also wishes to return to the Reformers. He has given impetus to the renascence of Calvin studies. It must also be acknowledged that Barth says he does not wish to form a new school of thought. He asserts that he is not a Barthian, and he rejects the term Barthianism. Although one can appreciate this concern, it can hardly be denied that Barth has in fact established a school of thought. Perhaps there are not so many full-fledged Barthians today as there were some years ago. At least in German-speaking lands there seems to be a movement away from Barth to the more radical theology of Rudolf Bultmann. Yet it seems clear that Barth has produced a new theology and to this extent has been the founder of a new school of thought.

In spite of Barth's appeal to Scripture, to the Reformers and to the historic Reformed creeds, his theology is not really in harmony with these writings. When appeal is made to the historic creeds, it is often to their words rather than to their substance. The claim to find support in Calvin sometimes involves a reinterpretation of Calvin in order to substantiate such an appeal. And it is recognized that Barth's exegesis of Scripture often involves an almost complete break with the history of interpretation. The evidence for these considerations obviously involves much more time and space than is available here.

The newness of Barth's theology and the actual break with the historical line is evident when one attempts to set forth Barth's thought in order to contrast it with historic Reformed theology. While one can contrast the Lutheran, the Arminian, and even the Roman Catholic position at various points with Reformed doctrine, it is almost impossible to do this with Barth's theology. The very foundation, basic framework, and entire structure of his theology is so different from the theologies of the past, that it is almost impossible to make such a contrast on various points of doctrine. One is required to set forth the structure of his theology in order to make some contrasts. The dialectical theology is a new theology even though it has roots in the past and similarities with other positions of today.

It is not possible to indicate in detail the newness of Barth's theology and its break with great Reformed theologians of the past. Just a few of the striking differences can be enumerated. Barth's view of Scripture has already been mentioned. His rejection of God's general revelation in nature and history is another unique difference. Barth's view of God has some resemblance to the monarchianism of the ancients, although his modalistic view of the Trinity is more complex than the earlier forms of modalism. H. Richard Niebuhr speaks of a "new unitarianism of the second person."[30] Barth's view of election is clearly divergent from that of the Reformers, and it appears to involve an implicit universalism. The Genesis account of creation is regarded as *saga,* and an original state of perfection prior to Adam's fall is denied. Barth's view of God's relation to the world in preservation and government is a new one in which an old Kantian distinction seems to be revived, namely the distinction between *Historie* and *Geschichte.* In spite of his emphasis upon Jesus Christ and his acceptance of a doctrine of the virgin birth and the resurrection, the complex distinction regarding history (*Historie* and *Geschichte)* makes problematic the genuine historicity of the redemptive work of Christ as the foundation for the Christian faith. Barth's emphasis upon the reconciling significance of the incarnation itself robs the cross of Christ of its biblical meaning, and the resurrection as *Geschichte* has hardly more than the revelatory function of making known that God and man have been joined in the incarnation. The

---

[30]*Op. cit.,* p. 250.

description of Barth's doctrine of reconciliation in the third chapter will demonstrate the newness of Barth's theology in further detail. His view of the sacraments as ethics and his denial of infant baptism may also be mentioned. In all of this one sees at least that Barth has not really returned to the Reformers and the Reformed confessions. He has broken with the historic Reformed tradition, and he has developed a new, complex dialectical or neo-orthodox theology.

3. Finally, we must attempt a brief evaluation of the desire to make theology a servant of the Church. Here too, there is a great difference between Kuyper or Bavinck and Karl Barth, although the desire was characteristic of each of them.

Barth's earnestness on this score became clear when he abandoned the *Christian Dogmatics* of 1927 and began with the *Church Dogmatics* of 1932. Since there is "no private Christianity," according to Barth, "theology cannot be carried on in the private lighthouses of some sort of merely personal discoveries and opinions. It can be carried on only in the church—it can be put to work in all its elements only in the context of the questioning and answering of the Christian community and in the rigorous service of its commission to all men."[31]

Historically, too, Barth's concern for the church is evident. It was Barth who roused many Germans to resist Hitler's encroachment upon the church and to form the Confessing Church of Germany. The creed of this Church, the Barmen Confession of 1934, was written almost entirely by Karl Barth. It must also be acknowledged that for many people the Church has received new significance through the influence of Barth's theology. He asserts that "we must, each in his place, take part in its life and join in its service."[32] The liberal idea of the church as a mere social organization has lost ground. Today there is greater emphasis upon preaching (proclamation) and the mission of the Church. Again, the contemporary ecumenical movement displays not only the influence but also the weakness of Barth's theology.

---

[31] *The Humanity of God,* p. 64.
[32] *Ibid.,* p. 62.

Apparently the content of Barth's *Church Dogmatics* has also begun to find its way into the sermons of ordinary pastors. In his recent *Christian Century* article, Barth expressed more pleasure in this fact than in the scholarly literature which his work was evoking. He writes:

> I am pleased by the report, which I frequently hear, that the *Church Dogmatics* is to be found in not a few pastor's homes, is read and studied (if sometimes only as a reference work!) and profitably used in sermons, instruction and counseling, and thus indirectly comes even into congregations that are far away.[33]

Although one may appreciate the effect which Barth's theology has had in some circles and upon some churches, the total effect has not been and can not be salutary and enduring. Barth's revolt against liberalism certainly influenced others to reaction also. The liberal theology, of course, needed to be rejected. The important question, however, is whether Barth's theology has really called men back to the inspired Scriptures and through the Scriptures to Jesus Christ as the only Savior from sin. Such a challenge alone will, by God's grace, bring about a reformation of the Church. Precisely that is what took place through Luther and Calvin. But no such Reformation has occurred as a result of Barth's theology.

Whatever effect the churches may have undergone, a real reformation has not yet occurred. The Barthian influenced churches are not strong churches. A lethargy still holds them fast. And the reason, I believe, is that the Barthian theology does not have within it the power to be a real blessing to the Church. Its unbiblical character, as outlined above, can not provide the stimulating power which is so sorely needed in the Church today. Barth's view of election with its universalistic tendencies and his failure to call the Church to live by the abiding principles of the Word of God leaves the Church in its lethargy. Barth's theology has not really unmasked the nature of man's sin as guilt, and it has failed to present a message that meets man's tragic need. Therefore it has not really pointed men to the Christ of the Scriptures who alone

---

[33] Vol. LXXVII, 3 (January 20, 1960), p. 74.

brings that life and joy which is the fruit of the Spirit of God. Only where the absolute authority of the inspired Word of God is heard and obeyed can the Church be strong and genuinely Reformed.

In the face of this powerful new theology of Karl Barth, we are challenged to present the message of historic Christianity—the glorious heritage of the Reformed faith—with new force and power.

Chapter II

Karl Barth's Doctrine of Election

Chapter II

Karl Barth's Doctrine of Election

Emil Brunner declares that Barth's doctrine of election is "the most detailed and comprehensive discussion of the problem in modern theology."[1] Another writer asserts that the volume on election (II/2) "may turn out to be the most important volume in Karl Barth's massive *Church Dogmatics*."[2] There can be no doubt that the doctrine of election concerns a crucial section of Barth's *Dogmatics*.

In the doctrine of election Barth's attention turns to God in his relation with man. Here the theologian's attention turns from the deity of God to the humanity of God.[3] The doctrine of election also constitutes the connecting link with the doctrine of reconciliation. And in the doctrine of election one has an illuminating instance of Barth's christological approach since it marks "the high point in his program of bringing every Christian doctrine under the normative control of Christology."[4]

Although Barth generally claims to follow the tradition of the Reformers, he frankly admits that in the doctrine of elec-

---

[1] *The Christian Doctrine of God, Dogmatics,* Vol. I (Philadelphia: Westminster Press, 1950), p. 346.

[2] *Union Seminary Quarterly,* May 1959, p. 55.

[3] Cf. the much discussed lectures, *The Humanity of God* (Richmond: John Knox, 1960). Note e.g.: "In this divinely free volition and election, in this sovereign decision (the ancients said, in His decree), God is *human.* His free affirmation of man, His free concern for him, His free substitution for him—this is God's humanity," p. 51. Cf. also p. 49.

[4] George Hendry in *Theology Today,* October 1958, p. 396.

tion he "had to leave the framework of theological tradition to a far greater extent than in the first part on the doctrine of God" (II/2, p. x).[5] Hendry, in the same article, speaks of this as Barth's "most radical departure from the theological tradition in which he stands." This accounts for what Barth calls "the greater anxiety" which the production of this volume caused him since he "would have preferred to follow Calvin's doctrine of predestination much more closely, instead of departing from it so radically" (II/2, p. 1).

Calvin's exposition and defense of the doctrine of double predestination was due to his unyielding obedience to holy Scripture. Repeatedly Calvin asserts that he teaches and defends this doctrine simply because God teaches it in his authoritative Word.[6] But today Barth declares that he must leave Calvin's doctrine of election because of what Scripture teaches. "As I let the Bible itself speak to me on these matters," says Barth, "as I meditated upon what I seemed to hear, I was driven irresistibly to reconstruction" (II/2, p. x). In a unique way, then, Barth challenges the followers of Calvin. It is in the name of Scripture that Barth calls for a reconstruction of Calvin's doctrine of election. Frankly differing from Calvin, Barth sets forth what he claims to be a genuinely biblical doctrine of the election of grace (*Gottes Gnadenwahl*). This election of grace he describes as election in Jesus Christ which must be conceived of as "double election"; and he even asserts that his doctrine is a kind of supralapsarian view of election.

Because of Barth's personal theological stature and because of his extensive treatment of the doctrine of election, as well as the peculiar nature of his doctrine, there is a new interest in the doctrine of election today. Since the doctrine of election has never been popular, and even among traditional Calvinists has fallen upon hard times recently, it is not surprising that Barth's form of the doctrine should have a certain

---

[5]The quotations from the several volumes of Barth's *Church Dogmatics* will be thus indicated throughout.

[6]Cf. *Institutes,* III, 21-24.

appeal.[7] Especially those who still cherish the Reformed tradition and the heritage of Calvin will show a vital interest in Barth's doctrine of election and desire to examine it carefully in the light of Scripture.

A. Survey of the Doctrine.

A brief survey of Barth's doctrine of election will enable us to see its new and complex features. Against this background an attempt will be made to consider in greater detail some of the major features of the doctrine.

According to Barth, election is primarily and uniquely the *Election of Jesus Christ.* Secondly, it is the *Election of the Community (Gemeinde),* i.e. the people whom Christ represents and who cannot be separated from him. And thirdly, it is the *Election of the Individual,* since the Community does not exist by itself or for itself but as a witness to the individual (cf. II/2, pp. 94ff., 195ff., 306ff.).

The first of these three, the *Election of Jesus Christ,* is the most significant for Barth's doctrine. The Jesus Christ event is the source of all our knowledge of God's election. From this source Barth concludes that we know that Jesus Christ is the *Urgeschichte,* the first, original, and primary thing that God wills. This idea expresses Barth's form of supralapsarianism. The election of Jesus Christ is also double election. Jesus Christ is both the *electing God* and the *elected man.* Double election is also evident, however, in the fact that election involves both grace and judgment, both a Yes and a No. According to Barth, the Yes is directed to man while the No is directed to God. In Jesus Christ it is man who is elect while Jesus Christ is himself reprobate. In fact, for Barth, Jesus Christ is the only reprobate. In Jesus Christ God has taken man's rejection upon himself. The God who loves in freedom is therefore not against man but for man. In this sense Barth contends that election is the sum of the Gospel, the whole Gospel, the Gospel in a nutshell. It is not a doctrine

---

[7]After Barth spoke to a ministers' conference in Germany in 1949, the response of some was that this doctrine of election gave them new joy in preaching. *Reformierte Kirchenzeitung,* 90 Jg., No. 10, May 15, 1949.

that he is ashamed or afraid to defend. Rather it expresses the joy and blessedness of the Gospel: election is the best of all words that can be spoken or heard because it tells us that God is for man. Election tells us that in his free grace in Jesus Christ God determines Himself for sinful man and sinful man for Himself.

From this brief survey it is already clear that Barth's so-called supralapsarian view of double election is strikingly different from Calvin's doctrine of predestination.[8] According to Calvin, predestination involved the election of some men and the reprobation of others. But for Barth the Yes and the No are really the two sides of the one election. The No is directed to God himself since God wills the rejection, damnation and death of Jesus Christ. But this No is in the interest of the Yes by which God chose election, blessedness and life for man.

After a long and thorough discussion of Jesus Christ as the electing God and the elected man, Barth turns to the second section of his doctrine, the *Election of the Community (Gemeinde)*. The task of the Community or Congregation is to attest the existence of Jesus Christ before the entire world and to summon it to faith in Jesus Christ. The Community, like Christ, is really one, but it also has two sides, namely, Israel and the Church. The Community on its one side is represented by the Jewish people who oppose their election, but who as Israel are the secret origin of the Church. Israel is a reminder of the disobedient and refractory people who are the object of God's gracious election. Israel reminds us, therefore, of God's judgment, of Christ's crucifixion and of man's sin. The Church, on the other hand, reminds us of God's grace, of Christ's resurrection and of man's election. Israel is destined for hearing the promises of God while the Church is destined for believing them. Israel is the passing form of the Community while the Church is the coming form of God's Community. However, in Jesus Christ these two are not really two but one, for in Christ the elect triumph

---

[8]Cf. my booklet on *Calvin's Doctrine of Predestination*. (Grand Rapids: Calvin Theological Seminary, Monograph Series III, 1961).

in the "gracious end" which Israel manifests and in the "gracious beginning" which the Church attests and exhibits (II/2, p. 259f). Since God has in Christ put an end to the finality of the rejection of the Jews, we have a witness to the ultimate powerlessness of evil.

In the third and final part of the volume Barth comes to a consideration of the *Election of the Individual.* He criticizes the traditional Reformed writers for being primarily concerned with the election of the individual. According to Barth, it is the task of the Community to witness to the world and to each individual in the world by telling him that in Jesus Christ he is not rejected but elected. The Community must witness to individual men by telling them of the objective fact that Jesus Christ has borne the wrath of God and that Christ is the reprobate. In response to this witness, men should subjectively accept their election and believe and live as elect in the service of God. The witness of the Community calls men to believe in their election and disbelieve in their rejection. They are called upon to believe in the rejection of their rejection, to put it in a typically dialectical fashion. Although these assertions seem to imply universal salvation, an *apokatastasis pantoon,* Barth sidesteps this dilemma. He refuses either to accept or to reject the theory. Universalism is a theory of the metaphysics of history, he asserts, and the theologian must maintain the freedom of God and refuse to reduce God's freedom to some theory. Refusing to debate such theories, the Church must rather proclaim the supremacy of God's grace, the triumph of grace in Jesus Christ and the impotence of human wickedness. In the light of our election in Christ, Barth declares that man's sin and wickedness are the impossible possibility of man's rejection. While the individual who is isolated from God is as such rejected by God, this can come about only as the godless man's own choice.

With this all too brief summary the main theme of Barth's doctrine of election is now before us. He devotes more than five hundred pages to the doctrine and many of these pages are in small print. It is not the purpose of this chapter to examine all of this material. Attention will be devoted here to the main lines of the doctrine with special reference to the Election of Jesus Christ and the Election of the Individual. An examination will be made of 1) the source or foundation of Barth's doctrine of election, 2) his view of God's decree and eternal counsel, 3) the significance of the election of Jesus Christ, 4) the election of the individual in the light of the election of the Community, and 5) the question of universalism in Barth's theology. A final section will present a brief evaluation of Barth's position.

B. Analysis of Barth's Position.

1. *The Source or Foundation of Barth's Doctrine of Election.*

At the outset Barth asserts that the source of this and every doctrine must be Scripture. Tradition or experience may not be its source. Although this seems to be the same view maintained by Calvin and the Reformers, Barth distinguishes his view from that of the Reformers in important ways. According to Barth, Scripture is not itself God's revelation. It is not the inspired and infallible revelation of God. Rather, he asserts, Scripture is the witness to that revelation. God alone can speak his Word, but this Word can not be inscripturated (cf. I/1 and I/2).

Aside from this important difference in the view of Scripture itself, Barth indicates that the basic difference between himself and the older theologians concerns the hermeneutical principle by which one determines what the Bible says. The older theologians also went to Scripture, especially to Romans 9 and Ephesians 1. But they did not *read* Scripture in the way Barth thinks it should be read. "The decisive point is the reading of the Bible itself. It is the question where and how we find in the Bible itself the electing God and elected man, and therefore that reality of the divine election as a whole which must shape our thinking about the election and form the object of all our individual reflection and speech concerning it" (II/2, 148). Barth is referring to "the christological basis and starting point for the doctrine" (II/2, p. 145).

Barth admits that the classical exponents of the doctrine of election did look upon Jesus Christ as the key, the center and goal of Scripture. He admits that one can hardly give more prominence to Christ than Calvin or even Thomas Aquinas did. But he maintains that these men did not properly relate their Christology to the doctrine of election. The question is whether there is "a continuity between the christological centre and *telos* of the temporal work of God which was so clearly recognized by the older theologians, and the eternal presupposing of that work in the divine election" (II/2, p. 149). Calvin did not see this continuity, Barth claims. He regarded "the work of God which had its central point in Jesus Christ" as one thing and "the eternal presupposing of that work" as quite another (II/2, p. 149).

Barth demands that the hermeneutical principle basic to exegesis at other points must also be applied to predestination. The decisive point of difference between Barth and the classical exponents of the doctrine of predestination is that Barth claims to look "to Jesus Christ, to his work as the revelation of what God willed" (II/2, p. 152). This so-called christological basis for the doctrine of predestination constitutes the crucial element in the source of Barth's doctrine.

There is naturally great appeal to the Christian in a christological approach. But what is its specific bearing in Barth's thought? We have here a particularly clear instance of Barth's approach. All of his doctrine is modelled after the event of Jesus Christ.[9] Barth means to say that from the work of Jesus Christ one must be able to conclude backwards to a knowledge of the whole will of God. "The order proclaimed in the work of revelation and atonement must be regarded and respected as also the order of divine predestination" (II/2, p. 174). Since Jesus Christ came to save men, Barth concludes that God's will is the election and not the rejection of man. The source of this knowledge is not the specific words and statements of Scripture, but the event of Jesus Christ in the light of which we are to understand all of the statements of Scripture. Hence he speaks of the "crooked path" the "many apparent hesitations and contradictions" (II/2, p. 15) of

[9]Cf. A. D. R. Polman, *Barth* (Grand Rapids: Baker Book House, 1960).

Romans 9-11 since he reads these chapters in the light of his understanding of the Christ event.

The concrete significance of Barth's hermeneutical principle of reading all of Scripture in the light of the Christ-event is the clear rejection of the doctrine of reprobation as it was taught by Calvin and the Reformed Creeds. Here one sees the effect which Barth's principle has upon the very words of Scripture. For how could one ever deduce a doctrine of reprobation from an analysis of the crucifixion and death of Jesus Christ? Obviously this was the work of grace for the redemption of God's elect. Christ bore the wrath of God so that the elect may be freed from the guilt of sin and the demands of the law. Through Christ's work they are justified and sanctified in the way of faith. Calvin certainly acknowledged that. But he also defended the doctrine of reprobation because he was convinced that this was the teaching of Scripture. The Scripture, whose center is indeed Jesus Christ, tells us what God has willed and what he does. It is Scripture itself which reveals Jesus Christ. His person and work are set forth and explained by the Scripture, as he himself declared (cf. Luke 24:25, John 5:39, etc.).

It is not legitimate for man to attempt an analysis of the life and work of Christ and thereby attempt to deduce what God has eternally willed. The work of Christ as well as his person must be revealed to us by God himself. And man is able only through faith to accept what God has revealed. If Christ's atonement was not a universal atonement, it is only God himself who can tell us that. And if God is to be truly free and sovereign, as indeed he is, then he must be free to elect and free to provide limited atonement, and free to reveal to us just what the significance of Christ's work really was. In spite of its appealing sound, the christological approach of Barth with respect to the doctrine of predestination is really a sort of natural theology based on Jesus Christ.[10] Barth's christological doctrine of predestination is in direct conflict with the very words of Scripture.

---

[10]Emil Brunner, *op. cit.*, p. 351.

Barth does indeed engage in exegesis of the crucial passages of Scripture dealing with predestination. There are long exegetical discussions of Romans 9-11. But exegesis of Scripture is not itself a guarantee that one's doctrine has been derived from Scripture. It is my conviction that Barth's exegesis of these passages frequently shows that positions previously derived from his central hermeneutical principle of Christology are "illustrated"[11] from these related passages. At this point one sees how crucial one's view of Scripture is and how basic this is for the doctrines that are supposedly found in Scripture. The whole of Barth's doctrine of election hinges upon his basic christological presuppositions with deductions drawn from the event of Jesus Christ. The source of the doctrine of election for Barth is not the very words and statements of Scripture, but the event of Jesus Christ. And it is *Barth's understanding* of this event which constitutes the criterion by which all the statements in Scripture relating to election are interpreted.

2. *Barth's View of God's Eternal Counsel and the Decree of Predestination.*

Barth's view of the decree of predestination also stands in contrast to the view of Calvin and the orthodox Reformed tradition. Here again Barth suggests a christological approach to the decree. Barth asserts that Calvin's view, for example, involves an absolute decree *(decretum absolutum)* in which both the subject and the object of the decree are unknown. This, Barth contends, involves a static view of God's relation to the universe so that, like the static view of an inscripturated revelation, God becomes the prisoner of his own decree. The decisive correction which Barth suggests is the substitution of Jesus Christ for the absolute decree with the result that the static is replaced by the dynamic, and all mystery disappears: what was unknown is then known. In that way, so Barth claims, all paganism is banished from one's view of predestination.

---

[11]The term is used by Berkouwer and Polman. Note that W. Kreck and Ed. Buess are also dissatisfied with Barth's exegesis of these passages.

Barth agrees with the traditional doctrine in so far as i asserts that by means of predestination God has "tied Himsel to the universe" (II/2, p. 155). But he immediately adds tha "we depart from the tradition when we say that for us there is no obscurity about this good pleasure of the eternal wil of God . . . because positively we must affirm that at the be ginning of all things, God's eternal plan and decree was identi cal with what is disclosed to us in time as the revelation of God and of the truth about all things" (II/2, pp. 155-156) The older view is accused of involving a twofold mystery since both the subject and the object of election were unknown Barth maintains, however, that because the eternal will of God is the election of Jesus Christ, we know clearly both who elects and who is elected. "The substitution of the election of Jesus Christ for the *decretum absolutum* is, then, the decisive point in the amendment of the doctrine of predestination" (II/2 p. 161). Barth expresses the "innovation" of his thesis more fully. He claims here again that the revelation of the will of God in the work of Jesus Christ corresponds exactly with the will of God itself. Hence the knowledge of the decree is rooted in its complete revelation through the work of Christ:

> The eternal will of God which is before time is the same as the eternal will of God which is above time, and which reveals itself as such and operates as such in time. In fact, we perceive the one in the other. For God's eternity is one. God Himself is one. He may only be known either altogether or not at all When He is known He is known all at once and altogether (II/2, p. 156).

What view of God's decree is involved in Barth's position? The rejection of the traditional Reformed view is clear. A decree of God fixed from all eternity and executed in time through the sovereign providence of God is regarded as static, absolute and fixed. In that view God is said to become the prisoner of his own decree. In its place Barth contends for a decree which is alive, in motion, activistic and dynamic. And that is provided, he contends, by substituting the election of Jesus Christ for the *decretum absolutum*.

In this light Barth declares that "it is now possible and necessary for us to make the controversial assertion that predestination is the divine act of will itself and not an abstraction from or fixed and static result of it" (II/2, p. 181). If according to the traditional view predestination means "something unchanged and unchangeable" then "in the form of predestination a kind of death has become the divine law of creaturely life" (II/2, p. 181). By maintaining this view of predestination, Barth declares that Calvinism is based on a view of God which "was pagan rather than Christian" because "it thought of predestination as an isolated and given enactment which God had decreed from all eternity and which to some extent pledged and committed even God Himself" (II/2, p. 181). According to Barth, the living God can then do little else than execute his decree or at best "wills only the effects of His willing" (II/2, p. 183).

The improvement which Barth suggests follows the analogy of human decrees and willing. When a king issues his decree, he remains the living lawgiver to explain and apply his decree. Furthermore, the decree of the king can always be "corrected or suspended or replaced" by another decree and sooner or later it will probably be replaced (II/2, p. 181; cf. p. 183). Barth suggests that we should view God's decree in a similar way. What Barth does here is consistent with his earlier discussion of the immutability or constancy of God. There he allowed for what he termed a "holy mutability" on the part of God. Barth maintains that while God always remains the same *God,* God is able to repent and change his mind. Those statements in Scripture which speak of God's "repenting" are not meant anthropomorphically but express the "holy mutability" of God (II/1, pp. 496ff). In this way Barth attempts to avoid making God the prisoner of his own decree and the consequent Deism involved in that conception (II/2, p. 182).

Barth at least recognizes that his "correction" of the traditional doctrine is so radical that he wonders if it is still meaningful to retain the word "decree." He thinks he can still use the term to express the constancy, faithfulness and reliability of God. It is not the decree or the will or counsel but 'God at all events [who] remains unchanged and unchangeably the same" (II/2, p. 182). The term "decree" in Barth's thought declares that God remains the same God of free love who can, however, engage in "holy mutability" while directing the affairs of the world. The term expresses the fact that God "*has* taken upon Himself a committal, an obligation, and that in perfect freedom (in the freedom of His love) He has decided to abide by it" (II/2, p. 183). Barth speaks of God's eternal will as his decree because there is "the divine law, and not an arbitrary divine power overruling the life of the creature" (II/2, p. 183). But the traditional Reformed doctrine of reprobation laid "too great stress upon God's freedom," and "in this context it came very near to thinking of this freedom in such a way that in predestination God became His own prisoner" (II/2, p. 183-184).

Who then is unchanged and unchangeable, asks Barth? His answer: "God Himself in His triune being as free love. And not only God, but God's decree, God's electing of man according to His own good pleasure, an electing which resulted in the election of man, and man's electing of God and finding of his good pleasure in God. All these are as unchanged and unchangeable as God Himself and God's eternal will" (II/2, p. 185). Predestination then is not an absolute decree, but it is "itself history, encounter and decision" (II/2, p. 185). It is this predestination which moves everything else and though it is itself unchanged, it is not unmoved. Rather, predestination is the movement from the electing God to the elected man and then back again from the elected man to the electing God. "This movement is, in fact, God's eternal decree. God willed this movement, willed it from all eternity, and continues to will it" (II/2, p. 186).

According to Barth, then, predestination, or more accurately, election, concerns God's action in time. It is not simply the active working out of what was eternally decreed.

> If it is unchanged and unchangeably the history, encounter, and decision between God and man, there is in time an electing by God and an election of man, as there is also a rejecting by God and a rejection of man, but not in the sense that God Himself is bound and imprisoned by it, not as though God's decree, the first step which He took, committed Him to take

> a corresponding second step, and the second a third. If it is true that the predestinating God not only is free, but remains free, that He does not cease to make use of His use of freedom, but continues to decide, then in the course of God's eternal deciding we have constantly to reckon with new decisions in time (II/2, p. 186).

In view of Barth's objection to what he terms the mysterious, unknown subject and object in the classic Reformed view of predestination, it is strange that he allows for an election which can be followed by rejection. "As the Bible itself presents the matter," he adds, "there is no election which cannot be followed by rejection, no rejection which cannot be followed by election. God continues always the Lord of all His works and ways" (II/2, p. 186). He asserts that the Bible speaks this way in Romans 9-11 and presents a view there which can not be reconciled with the classical view.

How can Barth's view of God's decree be called supralapsarian? Not only others have designated it supralapsarian, but Barth has employed this term himself. Barth clearly rejects the basic presuppositions of both the traditional infra- and supralapsarians. Precisely the point on which these two parties were agreed, that is, an eternal decree which precedes the foundation of the world, is the feature emphatically rejected by Barth. And Barth frankly admits that he can call his view supralapsarian simply because a motif in that position can, after various "corrections," be taken up into his own theology. What Barth means by calling his position a form of supralapsarianism is evident from this statement:

> In the beginning, before time and space as we know them, before creation, before there was any reality distinct from God which could be the object of the love of God or the setting for His acts of freedom, God anticipated and determined within Himself (in the power of His love and freedom, of His knowing and willing) that the goal and meaning of all His dealings with the as yet non-existent universe should be the fact that in His Son He would be gracious towards man, uniting Himself with him. In the beginning it was the choice *(Wahl)* of the Father Himself to establish this covenant with man by giving up His Son for him, that He Himself might become man in the fulfilment of His grace. In the beginning it was the choice of the Son to be obedient to grace, and therefore to offer up Himself and

> to become man in order that this covenant might be made a reality. In the beginning it was the resolve (*Beschluss*) of the Holy Spirit that the unity of God, of Father and Son should not be disturbed or rent by this covenant with man, but that it should be made the more glorious, the deity of God, the divinity of His love and freedom, being confirmed and demonstrated by this offering of the Father and the self-offering of the Son. This choice was in the beginning. As the subject and object of this choice, Jesus Christ was at the beginning. He was not at the beginning of God, for God has indeed no beginning. But He was at the beginning of all things, at the beginning of God's dealings with the reality which is distinct from Himself. Jesus Christ was the choice or election of God in respect of this reality. He was the election of God's grace as directed towards man. He was the election of God's covenant with man (II/2, p. 101-102).

Barth's so-called supralapsarianism roots, then, in the assertion that the divine predestination is the election of Jesus Christ. And since this assertion in its simplest and most comprehensive form is the dogma of predestination, we must now turn to an analysis of what Barth means by the election of Jesus Christ.

3. *Jesus Christ is the Election.*

"In its simplest and most comprehensive form the dogma of predestination consists, then, in the assertion that the divine predestination is the election of Jesus Christ" (II/2, p. 103). In these words we have the heart of Barth's doctrine of election. By recognizing Jesus Christ as the election, Barth claims to overcome the evils of the *decretum absolutum* as well as the twofold mystery of the doctrine. Jesus Christ as the *electing* God is not only the executor of election, but also its *fundamentum* or foundation.

Although this position appears somewhat revolutionary in contrast to the classic doctrine of election, Barth claims that he is simply following the teaching of John 1:1-2. These opening words of John's prologue mean that "Jesus Christ was in the beginning with God. He was so not merely in the sense that in view of God's eternal knowing and willing all things may be said to have been in the beginning with God, in His plan and decree" (II/2, p. 105). In an even more significant way Jesus Christ is "Himself the plan and decree of God, Himself the divine decision with respect to all creation and its history whose content is already determined . . . . Thus Jesus Christ is not merely one object of the divine good pleasure side by side with others. On the contrary, He is the sole object of this good pleasure, for in the first instance He Himself is this good pleasure, the will of God in action" (II/2, p. 104). In this statement we have also a clearer idea of the supralapsarian element in Barth's view as mentioned above.

Barth contends that Jesus Christ is not only the Elected. He is also Himself the Elector. If this were not so, Barth thinks we would be thrown back upon an unknown God and a *decretum absolutum*. "For where can it ever be disclosed to us except where it is executed?" (II/2, p. 104). When we commit ourselves into the hands of Jesus Christ we are dealing with one who is known.

> But of Jesus Christ we know nothing more surely and definitely than this—that in free obedience to His Father He elected to be man, and as man, to do the will of God. If God elects us too, then it is in and with this election of Jesus Christ, in and with this free act of obedience on the part of His Son. It is He who is manifestly the concrete and manifest form of the divine decision—the decision of the Father, Son and Holy Spirit—in favour of the covenant to be established between Him and us. (II/2, p. 105).

Barth thinks this position is so obvious in the light of Scripture, that he is amazed it has not been grasped earlier. He says he has found a trace of it here and there, but only in Athanasius was it given any real significance. In later history, however, the insight of Athanasius was again lost. "The fact that Calvin in particular not only did not answer but did not even perceive this question is the decisive objection which we have to bring against his whole doctrine of predestination. The electing God of Calvin is a *Deus nudus absconditus* [a purely hidden God]. It is not the *Deus revelatus* [revealed God] who is as such the *Deus absconditus,* the eternal God. All the dubious features of Calvin's doctrine result from the basic failing that in the last analysis he separates God and Jesus Christ, thinking that what was in the beginning with God must be sought elsewhere than in Jesus Christ. Thus with all his forceful and impressive acknowledgment of the divine election of grace, ultimately he still passes by the grace of God as it has appeared in Jesus Christ" (II/2, p. 111). In this strong opposition to Calvin we sense the seriousness of Barth's contention that election is in Jesus Christ.

Although Barth does admit that the Father and the Holy Spirit elect, his usual assertion is that Jesus Christ is the electing God. By means of this assertion he believes that the subject of election is made clear. And in this clarity the mystery involved in the absolute decree of God is gone also. When one asks who are elected, the same answer is to be given. Jesus Christ is also the elected one. All other elect are elect in him according to Ephesians 1:4. Barth adds that this is not "an illegitimate rationalization and simplification of its mystery" (II/2, p. 158). Rather it is the traditional view with its absolute decree that is said to involve a natural theology. "At root, can there ever be anything more unchristian or anti-christian than the horror of the peace which is given by the thought of the *decretum absolutum* as the first and last truth from which everything else proceeds?" (II/2, p. 158). Because the traditional view involves a mystery as to the object of election, all questioning is abandoned. "They think they know that we cannot know" (II/2, p. 160), says Barth. By regarding Jesus Christ as the electing God and the elect man, we "take away the idle horror or peace of the knowledge that we cannot know" (II/2, p. 160). The seriousness of Barth's contention is evident in the assertion that "the substitution of the election of Jesus Christ for the *decretum absolutum* is, then, the decisive point in the amendment of the doctrine of predestination" (II/2, p. 161).

We have already noted that election in Jesus Christ is called double election. Previously we have seen that the *object* of election is double. The name of Jesus Christ has a double reference since the one who bears this name is both very God and very man. "Thus the simplest form of the dogma may be divided at once into the two assertions that Jesus Christ is the electing God, and that He is also elected man" (II/2, p. 103). In so far as Jesus Christ is the electing God we must "ascribe to Him the active determination of electing," but in so far as He is man "the passive determination of election is also and necessarily proper to Him" (II/2, p. 103). Thus Barth holds that "electing [*Erwählen*] is the divine determination of the existence of Jesus Christ, and election [*Erwähltsein*] (being elected) the human" (II/2, p. 103). Thus God has "elected fellowship with man for Himself" and he has "elected fellowship with Himself for man" (II/2, p. 162). This may be called the doubleness of predestination with respect to its *object*.

But predestination is also double with respect to its *content*. Although there is a measure of overlapping between these two categories in Barth's thought, it is the doubleness of content that approaches the usual meaning of the terms election and reprobation. In electing fellowship with man, God wills that he himself shall lose while he wills that man shall gain. Or to state it another way: God elected man but he reprobated Christ. That is, the No of election concerns God while the Yes concerns man primarily. God has ascribed to man "election, salvation and life" while for Himself he chooses "reprobation, perdition and death" (II/2, p. 163). In so doing God "elected our rejection. He made it His own" (II/2, p. 164). That involved for God "a risk," "a hazarding of Himself," and a "compromising of Himself," or a "jeopardizing" of his honor (II/2, p. 163-164). This would be true if the elect man were simply a good creature. But it is doubly true since elect man is a fallen creature, the man "for whom the impossible has become possible, the unreal real, and the fulfilment of evil an actual occurrence" (II/2, p. 164). Therefore Barth asserts that "the justification of the sinner in Jesus Christ is the content of predestination in so far as predestination is a No and signifies rejection" (II/2, p. 167). This exchange took place on Golgotha. "There is no condemnation—literally none—for those that are in Christ Jesus. For this reason faith in the divine predestination as such and per se means faith in the non-rejection of man, or disbelief in his rejection. Man is not rejected. In God's eternal purpose it is God Himself who is rejected in His Son" (II/2, p. 167). When one looks into "the innermost recesses of the divine good pleasure, predestination is the *non-rejection of man* . . . because it is the *rejection of the Son of God*" (II/2, p. 167; italics added). And it is this, not because man does not deserve it, but because God did not will it.

One is led to ask, then, whether predestination is really double? Barth's answer is that the will of God in the election of Jesus Christ is "indeed double, it is not dual" (II/2, p. 171). By this Barth means that "it is not a will directed equally towards man's life and man's death, towards salvation and its opposite" (II/2, p. 171). For his starting point is that "in all His willing and choosing what God ultimately wills is Himself. All God's willing is primarily a determination of the love of the Father and the Son in the fellowship of the Holy Ghost. How, then, can its content be otherwise than good?" (II/2, p. 169). It is clear that the reprobation of some men, as Calvin taught on the basis of Romans 9, is rejected by Barth. "What," he asks, "is the supposed source of information" for those who hold to election of some and reprobation of others by a sovereign God? (II/2, p. 172). He answers that if our source of information is what God has actually done in Jesus Christ, then we will have to speak of a "disproportion between the positive will of God which purposes the life and blessedness of man and the permissive will of God which ordains him to seduction by Satan and guilt before God. In this disproportion the first element is always predominant, the second subordinate" (II/2, p. 172). He does speak of a "leftward election," but adds that "God willed that the object of this election should be *Himself* and *not man*" (II/2, p. 172; italics added). And thus he goes on to say:

> In Jesus Christ we can see and know this whole sphere of evil as something which has already been overcome, something which yields, something which has already been destroyed by the positive will of God's overflowing glory. And what it is in Jesus Christ, it is also in the beginning with God (II/2, p. 172).

Against this background of double election, in which only the positive element is directed to man, we can readily understand what Barth means by speaking of election as joy and not terror, only joy, pure joy. His view of election is one which excludes the element of the reprobation of some men. Predestination is the sum of the entire gospel. "For this order is found in the divine predestination itself, and it cannot be revoked. It is not a system whose component parts must each be considered separately. It is a way willed by God Himself" (II/2, p. 174). Again he says, "only the end affects us, only grace, not what God had to take away . . . by taking it on Himself" (II/2, p. 174).

4. *The Election of the Individual.*

Who is elected? We have heard that Barth's most basic answer is that Jesus Christ is the elected man. Jesus Christ is, indeed, the electing God, but he is also the elected man. Is there then no other object of election? Barth speaks also of the Community (*Gemeinde*) and the Individual as the object of election.

The classical doctrine of predestination was mainly concerned with the election of the individual (II/2, p. 195). However, Barth thinks the emphasis of Scripture does not support this classical view. Between the election of Jesus Christ and the election of the individual, there is "a mediate and mediating election" (II/2, p. 196) i.e., the election of the Community with its two aspects in Israel and the Church. Although there is a rather unique view presented of Israel and the Church, it is outside the scope of this chapter to pursue the subject beyond the brief survey which was presented at the opening of this chapter. We have seen that it is the function of the Community to attest the existence of Jesus Christ to the whole world and to summon the whole world to faith in Jesus Christ (II/2, p. 195). But the Community also has two forms as Israel and the Church. As Israel the Community represents the divine judgment; it is destined (determined) for hearing the promise sent to man; and it is the passing form of the Community. But as the Church the Community represents the divine mercy; it is destined for believing the divine promise; and it is the coming form of the divine Community. For Barth, Israel is connected with the crucifixion and the judgment, while the Church is connected with the resurrection and the divine mercy. In Israel man's unwillingness, inability and unworthiness is seen, while the Church represents the good-will, readiness, and honor of God. In this dual aspect the one Community must approach every man with the promise "that he, too, is an elect man" (II/2, p. 318). Thus the mediating function of the Community is to proclaim to each individual that he is elect in Jesus Christ.

When Barth finally turns to the consideration of the election of the individual, he again criticizes Calvin and the traditional doctrine for its predominant interest in the individual. Barth maintains that the main concern with man in the theology of Augustine, Thomas and Calvin was really the interest of humanism. This primary concern for the individual in the classic doctrine of predestination did not arise apart from "the earlier way of secular individualism" and it "paved the way for Pietism and Rationalism within the Church" (II/2, p. 308). This development went on from Rousseau, the younger Schleiermacher, through Max Stirner and Kierkegaard to Ibsen and Nietzsche, and it involves "the conviction that the beginning and end of all the ways of God, and even the essence of all divine truth, are to be recognized and honored in individual human beings" (II/2, p. 308).

It is evident that Barth seeks to avoid this kind of individualism by stressing the election of Jesus Christ and the election of the Community before dealing with the election of the individual. But Barth does not mean that it would be necessarily wrong to take up the individual first so long as one views this election in the light of Jesus Christ and the Community (II/2, p. 309). Simply put, election does indeed mean the election of the individual man. For "included in His election there is... the election of the many (from whom none is excluded)" (II/2, p. 195). The error of the traditional doctrine was that it was too exclusively concerned with the individual and consequently it did not say enough about him. Barth does assert that the election of the "individual" is the *telos* of the election of the Community (II/2, p. 310-311). Election is not the election of a family, nation, state or society. It is the election of individual human beings. And this, Barth contends, is itself an analogy to the Oneness of God (II/2, p. 314).

When Barth turns to the election of the individual, he does not set forth double predestination, that is, election and reprobation, as Calvin did. Barth's view does involve *universal election* (II/2, p. 306). Shortly we shall have to inquire whether it also involves universal salvation (*apokatastasis pantoon*). There can be no doubt whatever that Barth teaches universal *election*. He contends that all men are elect in Jesus Christ. However, that does not mean that all men live as elect men. Although all are elect, some do not yet live as elect, some may no longer live as elect, and others may do so only partially. But these possibilities–the "not yet," the "no longer," the "only in part or never"–are the possibilities of the godless man. Such a man, in spite of his election, lives as one rejected. To live such a life does indeed conflict with his election. But it cannot annul election since election is grounded in Jesus Christ. "The man who is isolated against God is as such rejected by God. But to be this man can only be by the godless man's own choice" (II/2, p. 306). Hence the Community must witness to the individual and proclaim to him "that he belongs eternally to Jesus Christ and therefore is not rejected, but elected by God in Jesus Christ; that the rejection which he deserves on account of his perverse choice, is borne and cancelled by Jesus Christ; and that he is appointed to eternal life with God on the basis of the righteous, divine decision" (II/2, p. 306). The Community must therefore declare: "In Jesus Christ thou, too, art not rejected–for He has borne thy rejection–but elected" (II/2, p. 322). Thus rejection may be attributed to an individual, but "only as a threat hanging over him, just as his election can be ascribed to him only as the promise given to him" (II/2, p. 321).

We have noted that although Barth speaks of universal election there is also a sense in which he speaks of certain men as reprobate or "rejected." In what way do these two differ? While the elect by their lives witness to the truth, the "rejected" lie against the same truth. The rejected are actually rejected elect. And their lying against the truth is really objectively impossible. They perform the impossible possibility. "By permitting the life of a rejected man to be the life of His own Son, God has made such a life objectively impossible for all others. The life of the uncalled, the godless, is a grasping back at this objective impossibility, an attempt to expose oneself again to the threat which has already been executed and consequently removed" (II/2, p. 346). Therefore the attempt of the godless or "rejected" man is evil, perilous and futile.

However, as Israel and the Church must be seen together, so Barth demands that the elect and the rejected must also be viewed together. The elect "testify by their truthful witness to what God wills, the latter [rejected] no less expressively, testify by their lying witness to what God does not will. Thus both serve the revelation of the divine will and decree which by nature are wholly light, but which cannot be revealed or recognized except as light and shade" (II/2, p. 347). In this dual service both the elect and the rejected reflect the two aspects of Jesus Christ who is himself both the elected and the rejected. "Believers 'are' the elect in this service so far as they bear witness to the truth, i.e., to the elect man, Jesus Christ, and manifest and reproduce and reflect the life of this one Elect. The godless 'are' the rejected in the same service so far as by their false witness to man's rejection they manifest and reproduce and reflect the death of the one Rejected, Jesus Christ. Because this One is the Elect and the Rejected, He is—attested by both—the Lord and Head both of the elect and also of the rejected. Thus not only the former, but no less indispensably, in their own place and after their own totally different fashion, the latter, are His representatives, just as originally and properly as He is theirs" (II/2, p. 347).

Barth makes clear that his reference to the elect and the rejected is radically different from Calvin's view of elect and reprobrate. Barth's view of the rejected must be seen in connection with his clear assertion of universal election. For this reason he cautions the Church not to take unbelief too seriously. "We cannot . . . regard their opposition as absolute. For all its distinctive sharpness, the opposition between them can only be relative, because both are in the one absolute hand of God" (II/2, p. 350). In the face of the rejected, the elect are called upon to recollect what they were and what God's grace has done in choosing them. And the rejected, on the other hand, are called upon to expect the same grace from God since Jesus Christ has borne their rejection too. The election of Jesus Christ reveals "the relativity of the opposition between the elect and others" (II/2, p. 350).

For Barth, then, election and reprobation do not root equally in the will of God. Election and reprobation are not equally ultimate. God wills election, but he does not will reprobation (rejection). Hence he speaks of "a number of individuals who as such are elect, designated and distinguished by God, and differentiated by their calling from the others; and in contrast to them there is a number of other individuals whose election seems to be called in question by the lack of its corresponding expression in life, or indeed to be directly denied by a contradictory expression in life, and in view of this we have described them as 'rejected' . . . . There are, in fact, these two classes of men, the called and the uncalled, the believing and the godless, and therefore the elect and the *apparently* rejected, the Community of God and the world" (II/2, p. 351; italics added). Barth admits that according to the testimony of Scripture these two lines are followed in human history which is "the history of the continually renewed consolidation, separation and encounter of these two peoples" (II/2, p. 351). But this contrast is clearer, Barth continues, where these two peoples are not two, but one and the same person, namely Jesus Christ who is the elect and the rejected (II/2, pp. 351).[12]

One then asks, who is the elect? "It is strictly and narrowly only in the humanity of the one Jesus Christ that we can see who and what an elect person is. It is He who is the man distinguished by this special relationship to God. It is His life which is the genuine fulfilment of genuine election. . . . If there

---

[12]Cf. *Römerbrief* where Barth asserts that Jacob is Esau and Esau is Jacob.

are others who are elect, it is a result of and in virtue of the fact that He is originally and properly elect, and that they are included in His election" (II/2, p. 351). And the rejected then? They too are most clearly seen in connection with Jesus Christ. "It is He—who just because of His election—is cast out from the presence of God by His righteous law and judgment and delivered to eternal death. In the genuine fulfilment of genuine election it is His life which is truly the life of the man who must suffer the destructive hostility of God" (II/2, p. 352). In view of the election of Jesus Christ "there is no other rejected but Himself. It is just for the sake of the election of all the rejected that He stands in solitude over against them all" (II/2, p. 353). And so Barth contends that the elect and the rejected are both necessary. "The elect are always those whose task it is to attest the positive decree, the *telos* of the divine will, the lovingkindness of God. And the rejected must always accompany them to attest the negative decree, that which God in His omnipotence and holiness and love does not will, and therefore His judgment. But it is always the one will of the one God which both attest. . .the covenant which comprehends both" (II/2, p. 353).

The activistic character of predestination means, according to Barth, that the elect and the "rejected" can exchange their functions. At times the elect may need to be censured while the rejected is worthy of commendation. The elect must live as one elected and not as one reprobated. And the rejected is actually an elect reprobate who must come to know of and live in accordance with his election. The many elect and the many rejected have the function of indicating the love of God in its twofold nature. Thus in their differing functions both are authorized to live "by the fact that God has loved and loves and will love this One, and them also in Him" (II/2, p. 354).

What then is the goal and content of election? To what is man elected? In and with Jesus Christ he is elected "to be the kind of man for whom Jesus Christ is" (II/2, p. 410). Hence he is elect "in and with the community of Jesus Christ. . .elect through its mediacy and elect to its membership" (II/2, p. 410).

Formal though it may sound, the unique determination of the elect is "that Jesus Christ and His community form the determination, goal and content of the life of the elect" (II/2, p. 411). In its concrete form this means "that the determination of the elect consists in the fact that he allows himself to be loved by God—to live as one whom from all eternity God in His incomprehensible and unmerited goodness did not will to renounce, and therefore will not renounce" (II/2, p. 411). God willed to love the elect and therefore he wills that the elect "allow himself to be loved by Him" (II/2, p. 411). Therefore election means blessedness. And whether he knows it or not, every elect individual is blessed. This blessedness includes "receiving, acceptance and possession" but it is badly understood if it is not recognized to include service "in gratitude for the self-offering of God" (II/2, p. 413). Therefore the elect stands in the service and commission of a gracious God, a calling which is not merely private but is an official calling to be an apostle. He must "attest, represent and portray that which God really is and does in Jesus Christ alone" (II/2, p. 415). And again the universal character of the election stands out. In view of the fact that God has "elected for Himself the necessary rejection of sinful men" (II/2, p. 416), election and rejection are not to be considered as two possibilities which are equally open to man. What must be attested is "God's election as the possibility which is basically open, and God's rejection as the possibility which is basically excluded—because it is excluded by God's offering of Himself" (II/2, p. 416).[13] Through this determination of the elect and his calling to service "the ongoing of the reconciling work of the living God in the world. . . takes place" (II/2, p. 417). In this way frontiers are crossed from rejection to election, for the existence of every

---

[13]Cf. also the following:

Unbelief has become "an objective, real, ontological impossibility. . . . Faith, however, has become an objective, real ontological inevitability for all, for every man" (IV/1, p. 747). "They can be only potentially rejected" (II/2, p. 349). "A 'rejected' man is one who isolates himself from God by resisting his election as it has taken place in Jesus Christ. God is for him; but he is against God." (II/2, p. 449).

elect means "a hidden but real crossing of frontiers" (II/2, p. 417).[14]

5. *Universal Salvation?*

A much discussed feature of Barth's doctrine of election is whether it involves an *apokatastasis pantoon,* a restoration of all things. In other words, does Barth's doctrine of universal election also involve universal salvation?

It seems clear that Barth will neither affirm nor reject the theory of universal salvation. He calls it a theory of the metaphysics of history, and hence thinks that it is out of place in a discussion of the freedom of God's grace. "We cannot venture the statement that it must and will finally be coincident with the world of man as such (as in the doctrine of the so-called *apokatastasis*). No such right or necessity can legitimately be deduced. Just as the gracious God does not need to elect or call any single man, so He does not need to elect or call all mankind. His election and calling do not give rise to any historical metaphysics, but only to the necessity of attesting them on the ground that they have taken place in Jesus Christ and His community" (II/2, p. 417f). However, Barth avoids the opposite statement as well. "But, again, in grateful recognition of the grace of the divine freedom we cannot venture the opposite statement that there cannot and will not be this final opening up and enlargement of the circle of election and calling. . . . We would be developing an opposing historical metaphysics if we were to try to attribute any limits—and therefore an end of these frontier-crossings—to the lovingkindness of God" (II/2, p. 418).

Barth rejects both of these alternatives because they are abstract and thus should have no part in the gospel. He brands them formal conclusions without real substance. Because God

---

[14]Cf. II/2, pp. 449 ff. for Barth's discussion of the determination of the rejected. God's will for them is different from his willing for the elect. It is a compassionate non-willing of God. There is no eternal covenant of wrath corresponding to the eternal covenant of grace. "Because this is so, the rejected man is from the very outset and in all circumstances quite other than the elect. He is the man who is *not* willed by the almighty, holy and compassionate God" (p. 450).

is free and therefore directs his own affairs, these statements are impossible. "We keep rather to the clear recognition that whenever an individual is elected and called, a new man is created out of the old, the reconciled world is fashioned out of the unreconciled, and to that extent, in secret, it becomes the kingdom of God and at the same time a new witness and messenger of the truth of the divine election of grace" (II/2, p. 418). It is up to God to determine what it means that he was reconciling the world unto himself (II Cor. 5:19). Hence Barth says that it is better to preach a rich gospel than a poor one.[15]

We have now seen that Barth refuses to affirm or deny the doctrine of universal salvation. It should be noted however that his refusal to deny this theory does not involve his actual affirmation of it anymore than his refusal to affirm it involves his actual denial of it. But does his position perhaps tend toward universalism just the same? Or does a consistent working out of his premises involve the doctrine necessarily? On this subject the debate has turned, though not always with sufficient recognition that Barth calls the theory one of a metaphysics of history which has no legitimate place in theology.

Berkouwer, who speaks in this context as if Barth actually rejected the doctrine of the *apokatastasis,* says that "there is no alternative to concluding that Barth's refusal to accept the *apokatastasis* cannot be harmonized with the fundamental structure of his doctrine of election."[16] In his recent much discussed lecture on "The Humanity of God," Barth faces the question of universalism and concludes by stating that "we have no theological right to set any sort of limits to the loving-kindness of God which has appeared in Jesus Christ. Our theological duty is to see and understand it as being still greater than we had seen before."[17] In this light Brunner's analysis is not without ground when he draws attention to the fact that for Barth the real decision takes place in the objective not in the subjective sphere. Thus the decision has been made

---

[15]In a 1949 letter to a ministers' conference in Germany. Cf. the appendix to this chapter.

[16]*Op. cit.,* p. 116.

[17]p. 61-62.

in Jesus Christ for all men. Whether they know it or believe it is not so important. "The main thing is that they are saved," says Brunner. "They are like people who seem perishing in a stormy sea. But in reality they are not in a sea where one can drown, but in shallow water, where it is impossible to drown. Only they do not know it."[18]

C. Brief Evaluation.

Our survey of Barth's doctrine of predestination has shown that his divergence from the doctrine of Calvin and the Synod of Dort is not minor. Barth spoke of the need for a "total revision of the dogma" (II/2, p. 339) and this is what he has produced. For one who believes that the position of Calvin and Dort is in essential harmony with Scripture, the line of critique is clear.

It should be noted first of all that there is a serious semantic difficulty in understanding Barth's doctrine of election. Since his view is so basically different from that of Calvin, Barth would have done his readers a real service if he had chosen new terms in which to express his position. Instead he has continued to use the terms of the historic doctrine although giving them new connotations. When Barth compares his view with that of Calvin, he actually does injustice to Calvin's position. Injustice results because his view involves election only, while Calvin's view of predestination includes both election and reprobation. As a result many facets of Calvin's doctrine of election are not given their proper significance. Thus Barth claims that Calvin's view involves an *Unknown God* and that election is not considered in the light of the grace of God in Jesus Christ. Even so ardent an admirer of Barth as T. F. Torrance voices his dissatisfaction with Barth's treatment of Calvin here.[19]

Thus when Barth compares Calvin's view of predestination with his own view of predestination (election), he does not sufficiently distinguish what Calvin says about election from what he says about reprobation. And when Barth speaks about

---

[18]*Op. cit.*, p. 351.

[19]Cf. *The School of Faith*, 1959, p. lxxvii.

double predestination, the element of reprobation really concerns Jesus Christ only. The term "rejection" as applied to men is only a potential rejection, that is, rejection in quotation marks. In this unique construction of a new doctrine of election, Barth has again given evidence of the great power of his mind. But he would have served the interest of clarity if he had used his ingenuity in order to introduce new terms. In this way he would have avoided the tremendous semantic difficulty present in this volume. He could also have avoided the inaccuracy and injustice done to Calvin's doctrine of predestination.

Barth's view of Jesus Christ as the source of the doctrine of election is also beset by fundamental difficulties. A correct interpretation of Scripture certainly requires the recognition of Jesus Christ as the center of the entire Word of God. Jesus taught this himself (cf. Luke 24, for example). However, Barth's so-called Christocentric approach brings Scripture itself into conflict with this supposed source. From his analysis of Jesus Christ, Barth is led to declare that Romans 9-11 are partially contradictory. And the Scriptural doctrine of reprobation is rejected for similar reasons. Here again is a warning example of the serious consequences of Barth's unbiblical view of the Scriptures. The impossibility of bridging the gulf between orthodoxy and liberalism again shows itself. Barth's view of Jesus Christ does not accurately reproduce the teaching of Scripture. Barth has made a crucial decision in declaring that Jesus Christ (rather than Scripture) is the source of his doctrine, and this is the root of other differences that appear in developing his doctrine.

Barth's objections to the traditional doctrine of God's decree have been noted. But it is Barth's view of the decree which does not coincide with that of Scripture. He does not really allow for a finished decree or counsel of God which was made before the foundation of the world (Eph. 1:4), a decree in terms of which God works all things (Eph. 1:11). Barth regards that view as static and thinks that God then becomes the prisoner of his own decree, just as he would be the prisoner of a book if Scripture were itself the Word of God. But Barth is not doing justice to Scripture nor to the historic Reformed view when he makes this charge. The static-dynamic dilemma is not valid. Scripture indicates that the unchangeable God never desires to change his decree. It is because he eternally wills that he is never the prisoner of the decree laid before the foundation of the world. In spite of this emphasis upon the freedom of God, Barth has not acknowledged the very use of freedom which God has exercised and which he has revealed to men. Scripture reveals that God has sovereignly willed his eternal counsel before the foundation of the world, and that God executes his decree in history. And if God has freely willed to reveal himself to men through a written Scripture, then we genuinely acknowledge the freedom of God only when we recognize the specific use of freedom which God has actually employed. But this is what Barth fails to do when he asserts dogmatically that God could not have inscripturated his revelation and could not have made a firm and all-inclusive decree before the foundation of the world and still remain free. And so in the name of defending God's freedom, the very freedom which God has exercised is denied.

A few words should be directed to Barth's contention that Jesus Christ is both the electing God and the elected man. It is probably true that some contemporary Calvinists have not sufficiently emphasized that God has elected us in Christ as Paul teaches in Ephesians 1:4. The relation of Jesus Christ to election is an all-important one. However necessary it may be today to retrieve certain motifs in Calvin's thought,[20] we ought to be extremely careful to avoid ambiguity in doing so. The genuine relation of Jesus Christ to election (Ephesians 1:4) is not to be identified with Barth's view of Jesus Christ as the electing God and the elected man. We have seen that Barth's view of God's decree is defective. So too we must avoid his unbiblical view of election in Christ. We are elect *in Christ* as Paul puts it. And Calvin repeatedly stresses this also. However, Scripture nowhere speaks of Christ as the *reprobate.* Of course it is true that Christ bore the wrath of God against

[20]His emphasis upon election in Christ, for example.

sin. But the efficiency of the atonement was limited to God's elect (cf. Matt. 1:21; John 10:14, 15; Rom. 8:31-39; etc.). What Christ did, he did completely and effectively for his elect. But in his sovereign counsel God decreed to pass by some men with the operation of his saving grace. And this biblical teaching Barth has eliminated by way of the declaration that Jesus Christ is the reprobate. Such a construction of the doctrine of "double predestination" may demonstrate great originality, but that is hardly the test of sound doctrine.

It is important to add that orthodox Calvinists should be careful to avoid an undefined reference to election in Jesus Christ. In the context of contemporary theology, this insistence upon "election in Jesus Christ" frequently includes a defective view of God's decree which was noted in Barth's thought. "Election in Jesus Christ" does not accurately reproduce Paul's teaching in the Epistle to the Ephesians if one rejects the idea of a finished decree of God made before the beginning of history and the creation of the world. It is important to recognize that election and reprobation in this eternal decree of God are not parallel in every respect. But it is just as important to acknowledge, as Paul teaches in Romans 9, that election and reprobation are both included within the all-comprehensive and eternal decree of God. God is sovereign in reprobation as well as in election, and both are included in the eternal decree. It is this thought which the term "equal ultimacy" of election and reprobation may guard, although it must then be carefully distinguished from the term "in all respects parallel." An unqualified rejection of the equal ultimacy of election and reprobation in the contemporary context too easily implies the ultimacy of election in a Barthian sense with the consequent absence of the doctrine of reprobation as set forth by Calvin and Dort upon the basis of Scripture's teaching.[21]

Does Barth teach universalism? The question has received a good deal of discussion. Barth refuses to accept or to reject it. But most interpreters are inclined to believe that his position

---

[21]Cf. my booklet, *Calvin's Doctrine of Predestination*, pp. 47 ff.

implies universalism, or at least that his unwillingness to reject the theory is difficult to harmonize with the general lines of his theology. There is a strange ambiguity in Barth's thought at this point—to say the least. It is interesting to notice that one of Barth's most basic objections to Calvin's doctrine of predestination is the charge that it involves an Unknown God. But this charge applies to Barth—not to Calvin. For Calvin the fact of God's sovereign election and reprobation are *known,* because God has clearly revealed this. But since God has not chosen to reveal the identity of the elect and reprobate, except in a rare instance such as that of Jacob and Esau, we do not know the identity of the elect and reprobate. Yet by divine command, the gospel must be preached to all men, and through this means God will effectively bring his elect to salvation. Calvin also stresses that the man to whom God has given true faith may be assured of his eternal salvation as he looks into the mirror of Jesus Christ. However, Barth's view of election really seems to involve something of an Unknown God. Although all men are elect in Christ, so that what Christ has done has been done for all men, Barth leaves open the question as to what the freedom of God might yet involve. Barth's leaving open the question of a possible universalism, and his refusal to affirm or deny this theory, seems to involve an unknown God. The frontier from election to rejection and vice versa can be repeatedly crossed and crisscrossed. In view of the freedom of God, Barth insists that we must leave open the possibility as to what will eventually happen. But this view of the freedom of God involves an Unknown God and is in conflict with Scripture.

We may add that Barth's view clearly does involve an objective, universal election in Christ. He emphasizes this so strongly that he urges the Church not to take unbelief seriously. In this way he minimizes the Scriptural warning against apostasy as well as the call to repentance and faith. The total impact of Barth's theology tones down the desperateness of the sinner's situation as described in Scripture. The message of the Gospel is truly one of peace and joy. And even the doctrine of election sets forth the joy of the gospel, for apart from election none would be saved. Although we must warn against sin and the dangers of continued apostasy with its terrible consequences, the main emphasis in preaching should certainly be the message of salvation in Jesus Christ and the call to repentance and faith in him. But Barth's doctrine of election does not do this. His view simply calls for informing men who are universally involved in what Christ has done. Hence the urgency of preaching is gone, and the biblical significance of the call to repentance and faith loses its relevance.

These objections to Barth's doctrine of election do not stem from a simple desire to maintain the doctrines of Calvin and the Synod of Dort. Our concern is to be faithful to God's revelation, the holy Scripture. Because of the teaching of Scripture, we must reject Barth and follow Calvin and Dort. It is not personal desire that leads us to accept and defend the difficult doctrine that some men are elect and others reprobate. This is the clear teaching of Scripture, and faithfulness to God and obedience to him demands our defense of this much maligned doctrine. In defending the traditional doctrine of predestination we are being obedient to Scripture and thereby we truly acknowledge the freedom and sovereignty of God who decrees according to his own good pleasure, who performs what he has freely decreed, and who freely reveals what he has decreed and does. Instructed by God through the holy Scriptures we must believingly confess with Calvin that

> we shall never feel persuaded as we ought that our salvation flows from the free mercy of God as its fountain, until we are made acquainted with his eternal election, the grace of God being illustrated by the contrast—namely, that he does not adopt promiscuously to the hope of salvation, but gives to some what he denies to others. It is plain how greatly ignorance of this principle detracts from the glory of God and impairs true humility.[22]

---

[22]*Institutes,* III, xxi, 1.

Appendix to Chapter II

The following quotations, presented in chronological order, provide a survey of Barth's views on the question of universalism.

1. Barth's earliest lectures on predestination were delivered in Hungary in 1936 (*Gottes Gnadenwahl,* Theologische Existenz Heute, Heft 47, 1936). Barth was asked whether one could still speak of reprobation since God is eternal love. Barth's answer was that "from ourselves we cannot know the love of God because it is not human love. We may not draw easy human conclusions from the concept of the love of God" (p. 50, cf. 24). The question was put in a slightly more forceful way at Debreczen: "Does not the universal grace which desires to save all men eliminate reprobation?" (p. 50). To this Barth replied: "We can be certain that God's lordship is and will be total in all, but what this signifies for us must be left to God. And therefore we dare not say that the universal grace of God eliminates damnation. The Holy Scriptures speak of election and of rejection" (p. 50).
   Earlier Barth said: "Therefore we cannot say: there are elect and reprobate. We can and must believe, however, that there will be such. We are on the way to this reality. That is our human life, that we find ourselves on this way" (p.48).
   In commenting on these statements, Berkouwer states that he finds nothing parallel to this statement in the *Church Dogmatics* II/2 (*op. cit.,* p. 117). When this quotation was called to Barth's attention at a seminar in Basel in 1960, he said that he could not believe that he had ever made such a statement.

2. The various statements on this subject from the *Church Dogmatics* II/2, 1946 (E.T. 1956) have been quoted in the text of this chapter. Cf. p. 462 e.g. There Barth speaks of the acceptance or denial of the theory of universalism as an indication of one's involvement in a metaphysics of history which conflicts with the freedom of God.

3. In 1947 Barth published another of his Theologische Studien, Heft 23, entitled *Die Botschaft von der freien Gnade Gottes.* Here Barth asserts that "grace will yet show itself more powerful

than anything which the children of this world can set over against it in their ignorance and disobedience" (p. 7). Does this mean then an *apokatastasis pantoon*? "No, for grace which would in the end automatically have to reach and embrace everyone and anyone would certainly not be sovereign, it would not be grace" (p. 7).

"Has Christ died for our sins alone? Has He not according to John been sacrificed for the sins of the whole world? Peculiar Christendom, whose most pressing problem seems to consist in this, that God's grace in this direction should be too free, that hell, instead of being amply populated, might one day perhaps be found to be empty" (p. 8).

4. In 1949 Barth wrote to a German ministers' conference (Kreck, Weber, Wolf) which was devoted to the doctrine of election. "Will you also find me guilty of the error of holding to the *apokatastasis* or will you be one with me in the conviction that it is always more advisable with this danger to preach the life-giving gospel than without this danger to preach the law that kills? Will the acknowledgment—however we may come to it—also strengthen you that the word of God's gracious election, is really a word of joy with which, as we face both Christians and non-Christians, we can both begin and end." Walter Kreck, *Die Lehre von der Prädestination,* Theologische Existenz Heute, N.F. 28, 1951.

5. The 1956 lecture on the *Humanity of God* (E.T. 1960) also deals with the same question in a similar way. After stressing the humanity of God and the joy of the gospel and universal election, he turns to the question:

"Does this mean universalism? I wish here to make only three short observations, in which one is to detect no position for or against that which passes among us under this term.

1. One should not surrender himself in any case to the panic which this word seems to spread abroad, before informing himself exactly concerning its possible sense or non-sense.

2. One should at least be stimulated by the passage, Colossians 1:19, which admittedly states that God has determined through His Son as His image and as the first-born of the whole Creation to 'reconcile all things (τὰ πάντα) to himself,' to consider whether the concept could not perhaps have a good meaning. The same can be said of parallel passages.

3. One question should for a moment be asked, in view of the 'danger' with which one may see this concept gradually

surrounded. What of the 'danger' of the eternally skeptical-critical theologian who is ever and again suspiciously questioning, because fundamentally always legalistic and therefore in the main morosely gloomy? Is not his presence among us currently more threatening than that of the unbecomingly cheerful indifferentism or even antinomianism, to which one with a certain understanding of universalism could in fact deliver himself? This much is certain, that we have no theological right to set any sort of limits to the loving-kindness of God which has appeared in Jesus Christ. Our theological duty is to see and understand it as being still greater than we had seen before" (p. 61-62).

Chapter III

Karl Barth's Doctrine of Reconciliation

Chapter III

Karl Barth's Doctrine of Reconciliation

Hans Ur von Balthasar, a Swiss Jesuit, has compared the structure and material of Barth's theology to the music of Mozart. He maintains that the "harmonious interweaving of themes" is nowhere more conspicuous than in the doctrine of reconciliation where everything combines "to produce the triumphant praise of the grace of God."[1] The doctrine of reconciliation stresses that God is *with man* in the fulfilment of the covenant of grace.

The doctrine of reconciliation constitutes one of the most extensive single parts of Barth's *Church Dogmatics.* Four large volumes have already been published and a fifth is still in preparation.[2] Barth does not deal simply with the doctrine of the atonement. For him the doctrine of reconciliation includes what theologians have usually distinguished as Christology, hamartiology, soteriology, and ecclesiology. Because of the comprehensive nature of the doctrine of reconciliation, Barth acknowledges that he is conscious of being at the "centre of all Christian knowledge" so that "to fail here is to fail everywhere" (IV/1, p. ix).

Many writers have felt that in his earlier writings Barth did not show sufficient interest in man and his salvation. It was thought that Barth's theology was almost exclusively a theology of God, his freedom and his judgment. But now the doctrine of reconciliation contains long sections on the justification and sanctification of man. It deals with subjective

---

[1]Quoted by A. Cochrane in *Theology Today,* Oct. 1956, p. 377.

[2]Volumes IV/1, 1953 (E.T. 1956); IV/2, 1955 (E.T. 1958); IV/3a, 1959; IV/3b, 1959.

soteriology in faith, love and hope. And therefore these new volumes of the *Church Dogmatics* have immediately received an unusual amount of attention. Arthur Cochrane predicts that this subject will "excite keenest interest among... practical-minded... activist readers in America."[3] John Mackay, former president of Princeton Seminary, was one who had been quite sceptical with respect to the place of man in Barth's thought. But he has now expressed a lyrical tribute to "Barth's loyalty to Christ's lordship and especially his growing appreciation of that lordship in its implications in the subjective realm of Christian experience."[4]

With intuitive perception Barth has predicted this favorable response to his doctrine of reconciliation, especially on the part of those whom he calls Pietists and Evangelical writers. But he adds, significantly, that he is sure they will not be "entirely satisfied, for at the decisive points they cannot fail to hear something of the rolling thunder of the 1921 *Romans* even in the more accommodating tones in which I now express the things which particularly affect them" (IV/2, p. x). And for those who think they perceive a new change of thought in the *Dogmatics,* Barth adds:

> But I seem to hear from one and another of my former friends and fellows the question whether in the aspect of the matter which is now to the forefront I have not gone too far in what I ascribe to man, rather like an old lion who has finally turned to eat straw . . . . Perspicuous readers will surely notice that there is no break with the basic view which I have adopted since my parting from Liberalism, but only a more consistent turn in its development (IV/2, p. x).

A. The Scope of the Doctrine of Reconciliation.

It is not common for Reformed theologians to speak of reconciliation as a structural part of the system of dogmatics. In the *Church Dogmatics,* the term "reconciliation" is the usual translation of the German word *Versöhnung,* which includes the ideas of both atonement and reconciliation. The English

---

[3]*Theology Today,* October 1956, p. 376.
[4]*Ibid.,* p. 291.

translators have had quite a time rendering this German term accurately. At first they usually rendered it "atonement" but by the time they had reached volume IV/2 they had adopted as the general translation the term "reconciliation" and employed the term "atonement" only for certain contexts which seemed to demand it. The extensive and complex character of Barth's doctrine of *Versöhnung* requires a brief survey first of all so that we can then direct our attention in this brief chapter to one aspect of the total doctrine.

The systematic structure of the *Church Dogmatics* is striking in the doctrine of reconciliation. Barth begins with Christology, and in its light develops the doctrine of reconciliation in all of its ramifications. In the light of Jesus Christ as true God and true man, Barth draws conclusions as to the nature of sin. Sin involves man's doing the opposite of what Jesus Christ does. Since Jesus Christ involves the humiliation of God, the exaltation of man and the prophetic setting forth of the truth, Barth concludes that sin involves the parallel aspects of pride, sloth and falsehood—corresponding inversely to what Christ does. Then Barth moves on to objective soteriology. The work of Christ involves the objective justification, sanctification and calling of man. Next he turns to ecclesiology, for it is in the light of Jesus Christ that the Church is awakened (gathered), quickened and sent. Only then is attention directed to the individual in subjective soteriology. The faith, love and hope of the individual is also seen in the light of what Christ has done. And, as if this were not complex enough, the doctrine of reconciliation will be rounded off in the yet to be published volume dealing with the ethics of reconciliation. And here Barth again makes one of his theological innovations by considering baptism and the Lord's Supper as part of ethics.[5]

In bringing the doctrines of Christology, hamartiology, soteriology and ecclesiology together, Barth contends that he has made many significant contributions to the doctrine of reconciliation. He believes that, true to his own christological principles, he has made Christology central and again given

[5]I had the opportunity of hearing the lectures on baptism in Basel during the school year 1959-1960.

it its rightful significance for the whole of theology. Objecting to the common distinction of Reformed theologians between the person and work of Christ, Barth has brought together into intimate relation the doctrine of the two natures and the two states together with the three offices of Christ. In doing this he feels that he has given new prominence to the prophetic office of Christ which was threatened with becoming the step-child of dogmatics. The doctrine of sin has also been given its rightful place, Barth thinks. He has made it precede rather than follow Christology for sin is known only from grace. This is Barth's answer to the question of the relation of the law and the gospel. He insists that the relation is one of *Gospel* and Law. Barth also considers it very important to separate the aspects of objective soteriology (that is, justification, sanctification, calling) from those of subjective soteriology (that is, faith, love, hope). These two parts of soteriology are separated by a discussion of the Church: thus the question of the individual again, as in the case of election, is the last question for consideration. Barth also asserts that this order, in discussing first objective and then subjective soteriology, is meant to be his answer to the subject-object problem of contemporary thought. He likes it to be seen as the view of existentialism turned upon its head. Then, as already mentioned, Barth considers it important to consider the doctrine of the Church prior to the discussion of the subjective aspects of soteriology in faith, love and hope. Finally, he regards as highly significant his presentation of baptism and the Lord's supper (no longer to be called sacraments) as the ethics of reconciliation.[6]

It is obviously impossible to attempt even a brief survey of the entire doctrine of reconciliation in this chapter. A representative selection will be made in which the reader may see the basic approach of Barth to the doctrine of reconciliation. The sections on Christology in volumes IV/1, IV/2 and IV/3 will give us such a bird's-eye view of the doctrine. Barth says this when he indicates that the christological sections stand

---

[6]Barth enumerated these items during one of his seminars in 1960.

"at the head and contain the whole *in nuce*" (IV/2, p. x). In these christological sections "the decisions are made" (IV/2, p. x). In order to consider the christological aspects of the doctrine of reconciliation, it will be necessary first to deal with the doctrines of the covenant and sin which Barth calls the presuppositions of the doctrine of reconciliation.

B. Presuppositions of the Doctrine of Reconciliation:

1. *The Doctrine of the Covenant.*

Historic Reformed theology could accurately summarize the Biblical message in the three terms of "creation, fall and redemption." This summary was meant to indicate that God had created Adam perfect and upright when he placed him in Paradise. Then God confronted perfect Adam with the probationary command of Genesis 2:16-17. And Adam fell into sin by transgressing God's command, breaking the so-called covenant of works. At this point God announced his plan of redemption (Gen. 3:15) and established his covenant of grace in which he provided redemption through the blood of Jesus Christ for Abraham and his seed. In place of the summary "creation, fall and redemption" Karl Barth speaks of the "Christian dialectic of covenant, sin, and reconciliation" (IV/1, p. 80). There is an important difference between these two summaries, and an awareness of that difference will help to see what is meant by speaking of covenant and sin as the presuppositions of reconciliation.

Barth does not speak first of creation but of covenant. He rejects the historical authenticity of the first chapters of Genesis. Although he acknowledges that these chapters do describe events or happenings (*Geschichte*)—in opposition to Rudolf Bultmann—Barth does not regard these chapters as genuine history (*Historie*) but as a Saga. The events or happenings are not those which happened once in a golden era of history, but they are events of Adam as representative man, and, as such, events that happen again and again. Hence Barth contends that one should really begin with John 1 rather then Genesis 1 in order to make a genuine christological starting point.

This conception of Genesis 1 to 3 as a Saga must be kept in

mind when attention is turned to the covenant of which Barth speaks. He does not mean the so-called covenant of works of Genesis 2:16-17 where we are told of God's entering into an arrangement with Adam in which God forbids Adam to eat of one tree and threatens death as the penalty for disobedience. Such a covenantal understanding of Genesis 2 would require an acknowledgment of the historicity of the record and a static view of revelation. Thus Barth even rejects the very possibility of a covenant of redemption between the Father and the Son as some Federal theologians have conceived of the eternal background for the covenant of grace in history.

> Can we really think of the first and second persons of the triune Godhead as two divine subjects and therefore as two legal subjects who can have dealings and enter into obligations one with another? This is mythology for which there is no place in a right understanding of the doctrine of the Trinity as the doctrine of the three modes of being of the one God, which is how it was understood and presented in Reformed orthodoxy itself (IV/1, p. 65).

According to Barth there is only one covenant and that is the covenant of grace. But this covenant is not to be understood in its historical context as the Reformed or Federal theologians have understood it in the past. The covenant of grace is not implied for the first time in Genesis 3:15 and then involved historically in God's dealings with Abraham and his seed. At this point one should recall Barth's view of the relation of Israel and the Church as it was touched upon in the previous chapter. The covenant of which Barth speaks, and the covenant which is the presupposition of reconciliation, is really the eternal will of God. "God elected man to a covenant with Himself, and created heaven and earth and man himself for the sake of this covenant" (IV/1, p. 68). In its simplest form the covenant means Immanuel, God with us[7] (IV/1, pp. 3-21). The covenant means "I will be your God and ye shall be my people" (IV/1, p. 38). And that statement, like election, has universal scope

[7]Cf. IV/1, p. 22, "The fellowship which originally existed between God and man, which was then disturbed and jeopardized, the purpose of which is now fulfilled in Jesus Christ and in the work of reconciliation, we describe as the covenant."

and validity: it is "for all men of all times and places" (IV/1, p. 39). But beyond this general statement, it is extremely difficult to state what Barth means by the covenant. Its immediate relation to the doctrine of election is clear. Because he rejects an original state of perfection, and does not distinguish a pre-and post-fall state of man, Barth's view of the nature and origin of the covenant is vague.

One does well, in trying to understand Barth's view of the covenant, to recall his early emphasis upon the gulf that exists between God and man. In his early writings he spoke of the infinite qualitative distinction between God and man. Although these terms are no longer used, the same basic idea of this gulf is present in his thought. Although orthodox Reformed theologians have always stressed the Creator-creature distinction, they have never done so in the way that Barth does. The fact of man's original perfection made covenantal fellowship between the Creator and the creature possible because God willed to enter such fellowship with his image bearer. Although it was indicative of God's condescending favor thus to commune with Adam in Paradise, it was not this Creator-creature distinction which initially demanded reconciliation. But Barth's view of reconciliation and the covenant assumes an original gulf between God and man which can be bridged only by God's reconciling action. That is understandable in the light of Barth's continued rejection of a *status integretatis*, a state of perfection prior to the fall. If Genesis 1 to 3 is accepted as historically authentic, then we see that God was able to enter into covenantal relationship with man without providing reconciliation regardless of the entrance of sin, for in his view there was never a time when man was sinless. However, the fact of sin does, according to Barth, determine the *kind* of reconciliation that is required to fulfill the covenant. And to this second presupposition of reconciliation our attention must now turn.

2. *The Doctrine of Sin.*

Reconciliation was necessary to bring God and man together. God's desire to be man's God requires reconciliation. It is for this reason, it seems, that Barth talks about sin as a *Zwischenfall*, an episode, something that comes between. Reconciliation was needed to bring the creator and the creature into covenant. But because of the *Zwischenfall* of sin, this reconciliation must take the form of an atonement. For this reason sin is also called a presupposition of reconciliation.

But what is sin according to Barth? He speaks of sin as a breaking of the covenant. By this he does not refer to the so-called covenant of works which is described in Genesis 2. In fact Barth speaks of sin as the breaking of the covenant of grace, for this is the only covenant. Man always sins against grace. What sin is can be seen only in the light of grace, that is, in the light of Jesus Christ. However, it is interesting to note that although Barth sets forth his doctrine of sin in its more complete form only after he has set forth the sections of Christology,[8] he finds it necessary to describe sin at this point as a presupposition of reconciliation. This is interesting because he criticizes the orthodox tradition for setting forth the doctrine of sin prior to its section on Christology. Although Barth does describe sin as pride, sloth and falsehood in the light of his Christological presuppositions, he must already set forth the essence of sin in order to make clear why reconciliation in the form of atonement is necessary.

Let us look more closely at Barth's view of sin. He holds, as we have stated above, that Adam was not initially perfect. "There never was a golden age. There is no point in looking back to one. The first man was immediately the first sinner" (IV/1, p. 508). According to Barth this is what the Saga of Genesis 1-3 tells us:

> The Bible gives to this history and to all men in this sense the general title of Adam.... The meaning of Adam is simply man, and as the bearer of this name which denotes the being and essence of all other men, Adam appears in the Genesis story as the man who owes his existence directly to the creative will and Word and act of God without any human intervention, the man who is to that extent the first man.... It was in this sphere of biblical saga that Adam came into being and existed. And

---

[8]Cf. each section in IV/1, 2, and 3.

> it was in this sphere...that there took place the fall, the fall of the first man. ...But it is the name of Adam, the transgressor, which God gives to world history as a whole. The name of Adam sums up this history [*Geschichte*] as the history of the mankind which God has given up, given up to its pride on account of its pride. It sums up the meaning or meaninglessness of this history (IV/1, p. 507f.).

This sense of the account of Adam's fall as Saga runs contrary to the parallel that Paul draws in Romans 5 between Adam and Christ. Barth's position is succinctly and interestingly set forth in his book entitled *Christ and Adam.* Professor John Murray's brief rebuttal is well put:

> It cannot be too plainly said that if we adopt this construction of Romans 5:12-19, we must abandon exegesis. If Paul emphasized one thing it is that by the one trespass of the one man Adam the many were accounted sinners and death came to exercise its lordship over all. Paul's sustained emphasis upon the one trespass and the one man, the one trespass of the one, is the very opposite of the idea of *repetition* upon which Barth's construction hinges.... It is this unique character of Adam and this unique involvement in his trespass that Barth eliminates.[10]

Thus by rejecting the historicity of Adam's fall in the biblical sense, Barth has been unable to set forth the true nature of Adam's sin which consisted in breaking a specific command of God by which he incurred guilt and depravity. Although Barth does speak of the seriousness of man's sin and also recognizes the universality of sin, he has not really acknowledged the true nature of sin and its actual entrance into the world. Scripture presents Adam as the first man who by his transgression moved from a sinless state to one of transgression and guilt. And when Barth does speak of sin as disobedience and breaking of the covenant, this has reference, not to the specific command of Genesis 2:16-17, but to some law of the covenant of grace (as Barth understands it) which demands that man must be thankful for grace. "Man is called to hold to the grace of His Creator, to be thankful for it, to bow to it

---

[9]*Christus und Adam nach Römer* 5, 1952 (E.T. 1956).
[10]*The Epistle to the Romans,* Vol. I (Grand Rapids: Eerdmans, 1959), p. 386.

and adapt himself to it, to honor it as the truth. And the essence of sin is that he does not do this" (IV/1, p. 140). Thus Sin says "No where God says Yes . . . In all its forms it exists and is only as that which negates and therefore as that which is itself negated, on the left hand of God, where God in saying Yes has already said No, where in electing He has rejected, where in willing He has not willed. But the divine Yes which sin negates and by which it is negated is the Yes of God's covenant with man which is the mystery of creation—the covenant of grace concluded in Jesus Christ from all eternity and fulfilled in time" (IV/1, p. 139f.). Sin is then "terribly real even in this negativity" (IV/1, p. 67), but it is also actually "the self-surrender of the creature to nothingness" (IV/1, p. 79). In the light of God's election and Christ's reconciliation, Barth repeatedly speaks of sin as an "impossible possibility."[11]

In spite of the emphasis upon sin in Barth's theology, he does not really regard sin seriously enough. He does not view sin basically as guilt in the sight of God which demands *satisfaction* if reconciliation is to be provided. And because sin is not recognized in its basic relation to God's law, the whole direction of reconciliation is manward. With reference to 2 Corinthians 5:19 and Romans 5, Barth contends that Paul is *not* speaking of "an enmity of God against man which is removed by atonement...The hurt which has to be made good is on our side....God does not need reconciliation with men, but men need reconciliation with Him...And the goal is undoubtedly this complete conversion of the world to Him" (IV/1, p. 74). Reconciliation is the conversion of man to God.

Against this background of the covenant and sin as the presuppositions of the doctrine of reconciliation, we must now turn to Barth's construction of the doctrine of the atonement.

C. The Christological Aspects of the Doctrine of Reconciliation.

In turning to the Christological sections of Barth's doctrine of reconciliation, we look at the most decisive part. Here the doctrine of reconciliation is contained *in nuce*. Here the basic

[11]Numerous instances. Cf. also IV/3 a.

decisions are really made. But if by reconciliation one understands the method and procedure by which God provides atonement for man's sin, he will discover little similarity between Barth's exposition and that of classic Reformed theology. Barth almost completely ignores the traditional theories of the atonement. Anselm's view of the satisfaction of God's honor is briefly mentioned but then rejected. The view of the penal substitutionary theory of the atonement is likewise rejected. In fact, Barth's strongest criticism is directed against the federal theologians and their view of the atonement. Here, as in the doctrine of predestination, Barth goes his own way. He blazes new trails and develops new doctrines.

According to Barth the reconciliation between God and man is effected by the Event of Jesus Christ. This can be summarized in three related statements, namely, that Jesus Christ is very God, very man, and the very God-man. Jesus Christ as very God means the humiliation of God and the priestly office. Jesus Christ as very man means the exaltation of man and the kingly office. And Jesus Christ as the God-man means his prophetic office. But there is no state corresponding to this christological aspect. A review of each of these three aspects of Barth's christology will confront us with the main lines of his doctrine of reconciliation.

1. *Jesus Christ Is Very God.*

The content of the doctrine of reconciliation involves the knowledge, first, that Jesus Christ is "very God, that is, the God who humbles Himself, and [is] therefore the reconciling God" (IV/1, p. 79). Barth gives a brief and pointed definition of reconciliation. "Reconciliation is God's crossing the frontier to man [*Grenzüberschreitung*]" (IV/1, p. 82). The description of this frontier (*Grenze*) reminds one of Barth's earlier references to God as "the Wholly Other." He says:

> The frontier is a real one. On the one side there is God in His glory as Creator and Lord, and also in the majesty of His holiness and righteousness. And on the other side there is man, not merely the creature, but the sinner, the one who exists in the flesh and who in the flesh is in opposition to Him. It is not merely a frontier, but a yawning abyss. Yet this abyss is crossed,

not by man, not by both God and man, but only by God (IV/1, p. 82).

It is in his freedom that God crosses this yawning abyss and thus shows that He is truly the Lord. God the Creator, the Holy and Righteous One, "emerges from the impenetrable mystery of His Godhead, which has become so dreadful to the sin of man, and gives Himself to man and to be known by man, to the one who has the faculties to receive and know Him, but has no will or capacity to use these faculties" (IV/1, p. 82). God crosses this yawning abyss by giving his Son to the cosmos and thereby God "sets at stake His own existence as God" (IV/1, p. 72). The profound love of God for the world of which John 3:16 speaks is really this "venture of His own self-offering, in this hazarding of His own existence as God." When one says that Jesus Christ is very God, he is referring to this "self-offering and self-hazarding of God" (IV/1, p. 72).[12]

The false gods, Barth declares, are not capable of self-humiliation. But the Christian message of reconciliation concerns the humiliation of God himself. Barth does not speak of the humiliation of the God-man. To say that humiliation concerns man is mere tautology. What sense could there be in speaking of man as humiliated? This is natural to man. But to say that God humiliates himself, that, according to Barth, is the real meaning of Jesus Christ as very God. Berkouwer regards this point of such significance that almost the whole of his critique at this point is directed to the problem of theopaschitism, that is, the suffering of God, in Barth's theology.[13] Barth puts it in another way when he states that in Jesus Christ "it took place that while maintaining His true deity God became man, in Him to make His own the cause of man. In Him God Himself humiliated Himself. . . . That is the secret of Christmas and Good Friday" (IV/1, p. 134). And it is this humiliation of God that Barth refers to as the priestly office of Jesus Christ.

---

[12]One is reminded of Paul's Tillich's idea that a final revelation must be able to negate itself.

[13]*The Triumph of Grace in the Theology of Karl Barth* (Grand Rapids: Eerdmans, 1956), pp. 297-327. Cf. also 125-135.

2. *Jesus Christ As Very Man.*

Under this aspect of reconciliation, Barth deals with the exaltation of man and the kingly office of Jesus Christ. There is a clear parallelism between the first and second aspects of Barth's view of reconciliation. Jesus Christ as very God means He is the Lord who becomes a servant. And Jesus Christ as very man means he is the Servant who becomes a Lord. The humiliation of God involves the exaltation of man.

What does it mean to say that Jesus Christ is truly man, *vere homo?* "It is the person of a true man, like all other men in every respect, subjected without exception to all the limitations of the human situation.... He is altogether man just as He is altogether God—altogether man in virtue of His true Godhead whose glory consists in His humiliation. That is how He is the reconciler between God and man" (IV/1, p. 130). Barth acknowledges that "it is something very bold and profoundly astonishing to presume to say without reservation or subtraction that God was truly and altogether in Christ, to speak of His identity with this true man, which means this man who was born like all of us in time, who lived and thought and spoke, who could be tempted and suffer and die and who was in fact tempted, and suffered and died" (IV/1, p. 183). Or again, "to say man is to say creature and sin and this means limitation and suffering. Both these have to be said of Jesus Christ" (IV/1, p. 131).

The fact that Jesus Christ is very man involves something of a transfer, a conversion of man to God. "What has happened in Him as the one true man is the conversion of all of us to God, the realization of true humanity .... As in Him God became like man, so too in Him man has become like God. As in Him God was bound, so too in Him man is made free. As in Him the Lord became a servant, so too in Him the servant has become a Lord. That is the atonement [*Versöhnung*] made in Jesus Christ in the second aspect" (IV/1, p. 131).

One can readily understand why Barth speaks here of the state of exaltation and the office of king. However, here it is simply the exaltation of *man,* while in the state of humiliation it was exclusively the humiliation of *God.* To say that God was exalted would be tautology according to Barth. "In Him humanity is exalted humanity, just as Godhead is humiliated Godhead. *And humanity is exalted by the humiliation of Godhead.*... In so far as he was and is and will be very man, the conversion of man to God took place in Him, the turning and therefore the reconciliation of all men, the fulfilment of the covenant" (IV/1, p. 131f; italics added).

Barth likes to express this exchange or transfer which took place in the atonement by referring to the parable of the prodigal son. Jesus Christ as very God is expressed as the way of the Son of God into a far country and Jesus Christ as very man is the homecoming of the Son of man. And he finds both elements contained in the assertion that "the Word became flesh." The following lengthy quotation indicates how Barth sets forth this parallel in his own unique way:

> There are two elements in the event of the incarnation as it is attested in John 1:14. If we put the accent on "flesh," we make it a statement about God. We say—and in itself this constitutes the whole of what is said—that without ceasing to be true God, in the full possession and exercise of His true deity, God went into the far country by becoming man in His second person or mode of being as the Son—the far country not only of human creatureliness but also of human corruption and perdition. But if we put the accent on "Word," we make it a statement about man. We say—and again this constitutes the whole of what is said—that without ceasing to be man, but assumed and accepted in his creatureliness and corruption by the Son of God, man—this one Son of Man—returned home to where He belonged, to His place as true man, to fellowship with God, to relationship with His fellows, to the ordering of His inward and outward existence, to the fulness of His time for which He was made, to the presence and enjoyment of the salvation for which He was destined. The atonement as it took place in Jesus Christ is the one inclusive event of this going out of the Son of God and coming in of the Son of Man. In its literal and original sense the word ἀποκαταλλάσσειν ("to reconcile") means "to exchange." The reconstitution and renewal of the covenant between God and man consists in this exchange—the *exinanitio,* the abasement, of God, and the *exaltatio,* the exaltation of man. It was God who went into the far country, and it is man who returns home. Both took place in the one Jesus Christ. It is not, therefore, a matter of two different and successive actions, but of a single action in which each of the

two elements is related to the other and can be known and understood only in this relationship: the going out of God only as it aims at the coming in of man; the coming in of man only as the reach and outworking of the going out of God; and the whole in its original and proper form only as the being and history of the one Jesus Christ. As we read in Ephesians 4:9f.: "Now that he ascended, what is it but that he also descended first into the lower parts of the earth. He that descended is the same also that ascended up far above all heavens, that he might fill all things." It is to this ascension, the coming in, the return home of the Son of Man, as it took place in Him, that we have now to address ourselves. This is the root of the second problem of the doctrine of reconciliation (IV/2, pp. 20-21).

3. *Jesus Christ As the God-man.*

Barth frankly admits that this third aspect of the doctrine of reconciliation does not really add anything new. In the two aspects of Jesus Christ as very God and as very man "everything that can be said materially concerning Jesus Christ and the atonement made in him has been said exhaustively" (IV/1, p. 136). The name Christ may stand for the first aspect and the name Jesus for the second. And all that the third aspect really does is to bring them together in the one name Christ Jesus or God-man. These facts "cannot be further reduced conceptually but only brought together historically" and "this is the new thing in the third christological aspect" (IV/1, p. 136). Consequently there is no new state to be discussed here for everything has been said in the humiliation of God and the exaltation of man. But there is a new office—the prophetic office. We are thus at once alerted to the major emphasis of this third aspect which is *revelatory*, a making known of what has occurred in the event of Jesus Christ.

Jesus Christ is the reconciliation because he is very God and very man. But Jesus Christ is also the *revelation* since he is both of these in unity as the God-man. Jesus Christ as the revealer or guarantor of the reconciliation means "that He who is Himself the material content of the atonement, the Mediator of it, stands security with man as well as with God that it is our atonement—He Himself being the form of it as well as the content" (IV/1, p. 137). That is not to say, however, that he reveals *information* concerning the atoning work. The prophetic office does not concern "the content of truth" but "the character of truth," that is, truth "which He Himself has guaranteed and pledged" (IV/1, p. 138). Barth is consistent with his entire exposition of the nature of revelation as encounter or confrontation rather than impartation of information. Rather what is revealed is that "as the God who humbles Himself and therefore reconciles man with Himself, and as the man exalted by God and therefore reconciled with Him, as the One who is very God and very man in this concrete sense, Jesus Christ Himself is one. He is the 'God-man,' that is, the Son of God who as such is this man, this man who as such is the Son of God" (IV/1. p. 135).

Thus according to Barth, Jesus Christ is not incarnate for the purpose of effecting the reconciliation between God and man through his reconciling death on the cross and his rising again for our justification. "Jesus Christ is not what He is—very God, very man, very God-man—in order as such to mean and do and accomplish something else which is atonement. But His being as God and man and God-man consists in the completed act of the reconciliation of man with God" (IV/1, p. 126f.).

D. Evaluation.

In turning to an evaluation one will have to reckon with the comprehensive scope of Barth's doctrine of reconciliation. In this chapter only the central thrust of that doctrine has been presented by tracing the elements of Christology or atonement. Although there is a formal similarity between Barth's doctrine and the traditional Reformed doctrine at various points, actually Barth's doctrine of reconciliation is a new doctrine in which older traditions and themes have been thoroughly recast. The interpreter will not do justice to Barth if he fails to observe this radical newness in the doctrine. And, of course, he will not be able to evaluate Barth's view in the light of Scripture if he fails to note the context of meaning in which Barth sometimes uses traditional words and phrases. Here I will simply attempt a survey of the kind of critique which I think Barth's doctrine requires. Each of the points mentioned should be greatly expanded in order to do justice to all that is involved.

It is not unimportant to note again that Barth's unfortunate and inadequate view of Scripture displays its influence also in the doctrine of reconciliation. I will not repeat the elements which were touched upon earlier. At this point one need only mention the relation of Barth's view of Scripture to his general view of history. His rejection of the historicity of the first three chapters of Genesis has been noted. By regarding this material as a Saga, Barth fails to adopt the biblical view of the origin and nature of sin and also fails to adopt the Biblical description of the need and nature of reconciliation. Since I have included reference to these matters within the analysis of Barth's view, there is no need to repeat these serious strictures here.

A complete evaluation of Barth's view of reconciliation would require a detailed evaluation of his view of history. Throughout this volume on reconciliation, Barth is engaged in what he calls a quiet debate with Bultmann. It must be granted that Barth opposes Bultmann's view which regards much of Scripture as mythical. It is also true that Barth allows for a much greater degree of historicity for the Scriptural revelation than does Bultmann. But it must certainly be added that Barth's important distinction between *Historie* and *Geschichte* does have far-reaching consequences for his view of the relation of God to this world and its history. While Barth's view admittedly has important differences from that of Bultmann, his view also has important differences from that of historic Reformed theology, and in these points Barth's agreement is more basically with Bultmann. Barth's view of God's relation to the world described by way of the distinction between *Historie* and *Geschichte* involves not only a view of providence (including preservation and government) different from that of Reformed theology, but also a view of the nature of the historicity of the revelation and the redemptive work of God in Christ which is radically different from historic Reformed theology and biblical revelation. But this is, regrettably, too large a subject for analysis here.

Furthermore, an adequate examination of Barth's doctrine

of reconciliation should also include an analysis of his view of the Trinity. A biblical view of the triune God and of the inter-trinitarian relations of the three persons of the Godhead is basic to a proper view of the work of God, not least the work of reconciliation. The fact that Barth should regard the very possibility of an eternal council of redemption as necessarily mythical is already very suggestive here. And his failure and unwillingness to distinguish the person and the work of Christ deserves further attention. It is true, of course, that the work of Christ is always the work of the person of Jesus Christ. Nevertheless, the distinction between the person and the work of Christ is a valid distinction, since Scripture itself makes this distinction. The second person of the Trinity existed prior to his incarnation and birth of the virgin Mary. The redemptive, mediatorial work was performed once and for all in history and it is now a completed work, a redemption accomplished, which is being applied through the activity of the Holy Spirit. Jesus actually distinguished between his person and work when he asked the question of his disciples, Who do ye say that I am? In this context in Matthew 16 Jesus indicates that a proper view of his person is needed in order to properly recognize his work. And likewise Scripture indicates that a proper regard for his reconciling and atoning work will require the recognition that it is the second person of the Trinity incarnate who performs this unique work.

It is not simply an unwillingness on the part of Barth to make this fundamental distinction and to recognize its validity. In the actual construction of the doctrine of reconciliation he so integrates the person and work, the two natures and the two states, that he ends with a view which destroys the unity of the two natures in the one person. In spite of his formal acceptance of the Christological decisions of the Ecumenical Council of Chalcedon (451 A.D.), his agreement is simply with words, which in their Barthian context have a significantly different meaning from what was intended in the fifth century. If, as Barth maintains, Jesus Christ as very God and the state of humiliation concern only God and not man; and if his being very man and his state of exaltation on the other hand concern only man and not God, then it is impossible to maintain the unity of the one person. And this is involved in Barth's rejection of the distinction between the person and the work of Christ. Barth's division here between the divine nature and humiliation and the human nature and exaltation is much more radical even than the early Nestorianism which was rejected at Chalcedon by the words "indivisible and inseparable." And not even the third aspect of Barth's doctrine of reconciliation in which he asserts that Jesus Christ is the God-man can bring about the proper unity of the person of Christ, since there is no state that corresponds to this aspect. The prophetic office, which indicates the real significance of this aspect of Barth's Christology, is mainly revelatory–making known what was accomplished in the aspects of very God and very man, in the humiliation of God and exaltation of man.

Closely allied to this fundamental criticism is another difficulty with Barth's view of the states of Christ. Classic Reformed theology usually divided Christology into the two sections dealing with the person of Christ and the work of Christ. The doctrine of the atonement (reconciliation) was then considered within the section on the work of Christ. Within this framework of discussion, the doctrine of the atonement concerned mainly the state of humiliation and the priestly office of Christ. While Barth admits that this traditional arrangement "seems logically very illuminating, and didactically useful," he nevertheless rejects it and charges that the traditional arrangement implies "a self-contained Christology" which "takes on the appearance of an ontology and dramatics arbitrarily constructed from Scripture and tradition" (IV/1, 124). This charge indicates that Barth's treatment of the doctrine of reconciliation involves much more than a new procedure in systematic discussion.

Barth's view that the two states of humiliation and exaltation do no follow each other in time, but stand along side of each other, involves a radical point of departure from biblical and Reformed theology. His view of history is reflected in this contention also. According to Barth the incarnation is not a means to an end, but an end in itself. And even the incarnation itself is regarded in an activistic way which means it is an event which constantly reoccurs. That is one of the reasons for Barth's unwillingness to distinguish the person and work of Christ. Not only is Barth unable to view the God-man, the one person of the incarnate Christ, as subject of both states, but he also fails to recognize the crucial significance of the cross and the turning-point in Christ's work when he cried out with a loud voice, It is finished. In fact, in Barth's view the incarnation is the really crucial thing in reconciliation by which the gulf between God and man is bridged. The movement from incarnation through suffering and death on the cross is little more than revelatory of the depth of the humiliation resulting from God's becoming his own opposite as man. The biblical emphasis upon our being reconciled to God through the death of his Son (Romans 5:10, Col. 1:22) and his having made peace through the blood of his cross (Col. 1:20, Eph. 2:16) does not really fit into Barth's doctrine of reconciliation. The cross and especially the resurrection have essentially only revelatory significance, since they reveal the reconciliation that occurs through the incarnation, that is, through God's becoming man so that man may thereby be exalted.

In using the terms "substitution" and "exchange" Barth is employing terminology that is germane to the Reformed view of the atonement. However, here too the context of discussion gives these terms a meaning quite different from the historic Reformed conception. The substitution of which Barth speaks is not that which involves a covenantal relation of Adam to his posterity and of Christ to the elect. The exchange that occurs is not an exchange which involves the imputation of Adam's sin to Christ and the imputation of Christ's righteousness to the elect. Barth does not view the atonement and the doctrine of reconciliation at all in the basic categories of satisfaction of God's law and of covenantal, federal, forensic relationship. For Barth the fact of God's becoming man by itself involves man's exaltation. The humiliation of God is *per se* the exaltation of man, and this fact is simply revealed in the cross and resurrection. This exchange, in the context of Barth's thought, is more basically related to the realistic theories of the atonement than to the Reformed, federal or covenantal views.

The universalistic character of Barth's doctrine of election is closely paralleled in his view of reconciliation. Objectively he can say that all are reconciled in Jesus Christ. Indeed, objectively all are likewise justified and sanctified as well. The same problems are involved here as are involved in his doctrine of election. The subjective aspects of faith, love and hope are primarily noetic: they involve mere acknowledgment, a coming to know what one already is through the ontic and objective work of Jesus Christ. The apparent implications of this view for universal salvation presents the same problem of Barth's unwillingness either explicitly to accept or reject this position. But the implications of his basic position, and the problems which it raises for evangelism and missions are again evident.

In conclusion it must be said that Barth's doctrine of reconciliation, comprehensive, complex and challenging as it is, does not retain the simplicity and truth of the Gospel which sets forth the centrality of the cross of Jesus Christ as the way of reconciliation and peace with God. It is an amazing fact in the history of doctrine, that the Church and her theologians were so slow in presenting a satisfactory doctrine of the atonement. Although there was certainly an awareness on the part of true believers, even in the ancient church, that salvation was through the blood of Jesus Christ alone, yet it was not until the time of the Reformation that the doctrine was developed in a satisfactory theological way in harmony with Scripture. Barth's view of reconciliation is one which again abandons these basic Reformed and Scriptural principles of the atonement. For Barth it is really the incarnation which achieves reconciliation between God and man. This motif, however, is not new. It has shown itself in various ways already in the ancient church, especially among the Greek Fathers, and it has reappeared in a variety of ways ever since then. Although this view in itself does great injustice to the death and resurrection of Jesus Christ, Barth's doctrine has further weaknesses in his presentation both of the states as well as the person of Christ.

We may conclude by repeating that in spite of his very impressive effort at reconstructing the doctrine of reconciliation within a framework seemingly Reformed, Barth has discarded the most basic elements of the Reformed view. Thereby he has discarded the simplicity and the glory of the gospel which Paul sets forth when he says: "While we were enemies, we were *reconciled* to God through the *death* of His Son" (Rom. 5:10).